Stop the Empty Search

COME FACE TO FACE WITH THE
REAL HIGHER POWER

A Memoir

LYNN K MURPHY

Copyright © 2024 Lynn K Murphy. All rights reserved.

All rights reserved. No part of this publication may be reproduced, distributed, or transmitted in any form or by any means, including photocopying, recording, or other electronic or mechanical methods, without the prior written permission of the publisher, except in the case of brief quotations embodied in critical reviews and certain other noncommercial uses permitted by copyright law.

Amplified Bible, Classic Edition (AMPC) Copyright © 1954, 1958, 1962, 1964, 1965, 1987 by The Lockman Foundation

New International Version (NIV) Holy Bible, New International Version®, NIV® Copyright ©1973, 1978, 1984, 2011 by Biblica, Inc.® Used by permission. All rights reserved worldwide

ISBN Paperback: 979-8-89316-685-9
ISBN eBook: 979-8-89316-684-2

DEDICATION

To my husband, Danny, whose love and belief never wavered. Your joy is contagious. Your example of service and sobriety changed me. To Sue, my sponsor and inspiration who listens and understands and loves me. And to those who find themselves in similar circumstances as me, this book is for you. I hope it will give you clarity, understanding, hope, and real answers because you are worth it.

"The knowledge that you have emerged wiser and stronger from setbacks means that you are ever after secure in your ability to survive. You will never truly know yourself or the strength of your relationships until both have been tested by adversity. Such knowledge is a true gift for all that is painfully won, and it has been worth more than any qualification I've ever earned."

–J.K. Rowling ("10 Rules for Success")

CONTENTS

Foreword ix
Author's Note xiii
Famous xv

Chapter 1:   Titles 1
Chapter 2:   Parents 6
Chapter 3:   Sisters 21
Chapter 4:   Wife 39
Chapter 5:   Parenting 54
Chapter 6:   The Codependent 64
Chapter 7:   Men 77
Chapter 8:   Career (Teacher) 90
Chapter 9:   Alcohol (Substance Abuse) 98
Chapter 10: Remarriage 122
Chapter 11: Church 135
Chapter 12: The Higher Power 144

Appendix A: Repentance, Sorry, or Restitution? 169
Acknowledgments 173
About the Author 177

FOREWORD

By Sue Alexander

I was drawn to Lynn immediately because of her grace, intelligence, and big laugh.

I want to share about many parts of this book, but I will share what is most important to me.

Lynn shares about her painful relationship with her four children. She describes it factually with curiosity, compassion, and insight and places no blame. She now accepts them as they are but hopes for the day when they will know the truth and that it will set them free. She wants her heart to be a soft landing for them all.

Growing up, she, as the oldest of four sisters, had all the responsibility. It was not easy or fun, but she loved them and wanted to fulfill her parents' expectations. She loved her parents with her whole heart and wanted to please them but "performance" became her main avenue to receiving love. She carried this compulsion into adulthood. It interfered with her getting to know her true self.

Her first marriage was a mistake. Her ex-husband filled all the squares she was taught to focus on–education and financial security. The observation of his family's emotional disconnectedness and his lack of vulnerability and openness got put on her back plate. She paid a hefty price for that. But she performed as she was taught. They stayed married for 26 years. When curiosity is present and peace is not, pay attention.

Lynn found her way to her intended career through ambition, forging smart connections, and a little luck. She is a public high school teacher. She has earned a bachelor's degree in economics and business, a masters in education, and a teaching credential in English. She believes that she was gifted by God to teach. Her fortunate students enthusiastically agree. I was with her when a former student met her unexpectedly in a restaurant. The look on his face and the huge embrace said it all. This happens regularly to her, and it is a joy to observe.

Alcohol eventually became a key to freedom. It did not flare up until her marriage difficulties became impossible to ignore. Her dependency had taken root and had crossed that line–the line that means you have lost the power of choice.

Her boyfriend, now husband, took her hand and introduced her to his recovering family of friends. This was pivotal for her. Listening to sober men and women deal with life, she decided not to drink. She needed human connection and love. Danny was the angel who took her hand and walked her lovingly into a community of people she now knows, loves, and wants to always stay closely connected to. Her obsession to drink was removed in 2017.

Lynn reaches out to newcomers in recovery often and eagerly–offering time, love, and lessons learned. She is a giver. She always makes time for someone in pain. She is loved by many.

Suffering produces perseverance and hope. Life is full of unresolved problems. She does it with the help of God. Her search is over.

Her book is going to have a big, positive effect on those lucky enough to have read it.

I love this woman!

Sue Alexander

AUTHOR'S NOTE

This story is not about religion. Neither is it about recovery or resentment. In it, there are many people and references. I, the author, dispute any correlation, positive or negative, between the above. It is simply my experience, and I am not speaking for any group as a whole.

I have consulted emails, messages, posts, journal entries, notes, and memories and have talked with several of the people who appear in this book in order to construct this memoir. To protect the identity of some of the individuals in this book, I've changed the names while remaining faithful to what happened as I conceptualized or experienced it.

FAMOUS

Ecclesiastes 3
A Time for Everything
"There is a time for everything,
and a season for every activity under the heavens:
a time to be born and a time to die,
a time to plant and a time to uproot,
a time to kill and a time to heal,
a time to tear down and a time to build,
a time to weep and a time to laugh,
a time to mourn and a time to dance,
a time to scatter stones and a time to gather them,
a time to embrace and a time to refrain from embracing,
a time to search and a time to give up,
a time to keep and a time to throw away,
a time to tear and a time to mend,
a time to be silent and a time to speak,
a time to love and a time to hate,
a time for war and a time for peace."

What do workers gain from their toil? I have seen the burden God has laid on the human race. **He has made everything beautiful in its time.** He has also set eternity in the human heart; yet no one can fathom what God has done from beginning to end. I know that there is nothing better for people than to be happy and to do good while they live. That each of them may eat and drink, and find satisfaction in all their toil—this is the gift of God. I know that everything God does will endure forever; nothing can be added to it and nothing taken from it. God does it so that people will fear him."

"He has made everything beautiful in its time." This is one of my favorite go-to verses in the Old Testament. I used to have it pinned up in my college dorm room on a vision board. It was often hard for me to trust. It is no wonder that I had to learn this. It was a verse that I wanted to believe but had to live out much of my life to get it.

CHAPTER 1

Titles

Daughter. Sister. Wife. Mother. Ex-wife. Redeemed Wife. Teacher. Codependent. Alcoholic.

Titles. Roles. Positions. What do they mean? To the world? To me? To you? Do they define us? Maybe. Maybe not. If not, then who or what does? More importantly, what purpose do they serve? Are they significant?

Higher Power ... now that is a significant title no matter what background we have. This book is hopefully a means to uncover more of this powerful and profound title. It is my quest for discovery and how I learned to overcome and become empowered.

When is it ever *time* to write a book? So many people aspire to write, and yet few who say they want to actually have the courage to do so. I've read and listened to a number of well-known authors who share that this is true. I know this because I have wrestled for many years. Until the last few years, when I began to become curious enough about actually doing it. I kept it like a locket holds a key. I wanted to open it and write what I knew was in my heart and what many encouraged me to do, but I have been afraid to write. So many doubts arise: What will people think? Will it cause anger? Will it help? Will it bring clarity? Meaning?

It's one thing to write for a class or a teacher. That is just academic writing. It can be taught and tutored. It is one thing to write a professional email; just Google it or ask AI. It is another thing to write a love letter as it puts words to feelings that are often treasured. It takes vulnerability, but it can be a game-changer in a relationship. It is a wholly different task to write a book that exposes the writer to the criticism of family, friends, and strangers.

Actually, I even needed to buy a book called *The Courage to Write* by Ralph Keyes to see if I could learn from other authors how to muster the courage to start and finish this book. Clearly, if you are in possession of this book and want to write, it helped me.

Then, I needed to read a book called *Finding Your Own North Star: Claiming the Life You Were Meant to Live* by Martha Beck. What a fantastic work it was to literally find that my North Star is teaching. And by writing, I teach from my experiences. This furthered my course toward writing.

Finally, and perhaps the greatest last motivator, was reading Anne Lamott, especially her book, *Almost Everything*, and her chapter in it titled "Writing." "Writing almost always goes badly for everyone..." It caught my attention. As I read on, Lamott stated, "If you do stick with writing, you will get better, and you can start to learn the important lessons: who you really are, and how all of us can live in the face of death, and how important it is to pay attention to life, moment by moment, which is why you are here."[1] She says a lot more, and my annotated chapter of her skilled words helped me realize that, at my age, perhaps more than half-way through my life, I better get "my butt in the chair" and stop thinking that what I want to write, what I care about, that needs me to tell it. I have a story to tell. It is the workings of the heart to write. It is a debt of honor. And I love to write.

I've had a folder titled "My Book" for years. It has stuff in it. Ideas on paper that I thought might make their way into "My Book." But nothing came from that file. Nothing. Except that I needed to write. I really wanted to write.

Something came from this idea where I least expected it and least wanted to expose my life's struggles. Some within myself, some outside myself. It's been like a puzzle—the kind of puzzle we call "Dot-to-Dot." The picture of the puzzle is unrecognizable until after the dots are numerically connected. But to understand the dot-to-dot puzzle, I needed to get from 1–2, 2–3, 3–4, and so on. Through my roles, my various titles, and my experiences, I found my

---

[1] Lamott, Anne. *Almost Everything*. Riverhead Books, 2018. p. 208.

reason to write. But it needed to have a reason to be read, too.

So, I'm guessing that you are reading this book, *Stop the Empty Search*, because maybe you want to know what it is like to consider finding or firing your Higher Power and to then consider redefining your Higher Power. Or maybe to help you understand why we need to search for one. What if the void you've been trying to fill (as I did) actually can be filled?

It is my experience that everyone I meet, at some point, is seeking to fill this void, whether they see that or not. It is being sought. The seeking is both personal and optional, intentional and unintentional.

The void. Maybe you feel like you were born with an emptiness, and/or as life progresses, you've been left empty-handed one more time in your seeking and wonder what it is all about. Maybe you are just curious about the title. It doesn't matter. If you are holding this or listening to it being read, I'd like to share what my journey looked like and why this may be a book for you. I hope it is. Because for me, if I am going to read a book, I need to connect to it and get something out of it for me, for my life. That is my reason for reading. I believe if you find yourself in any of the roles I have in the Table of Contents and you are even remotely thinking that you want to stop the search for a HP and want to define that, or at least put some arms around it and maybe some legs, read on. I tried and tried for years.

As I tell it, I picture myself sitting with you in a coffee corner or on my L-shaped couch cozy with warm mugs in hand, a posture of sweet presence, and my ears in tune with not just what is said but the details strained out, and the most important parts heard, and, more importantly, understood. But, if it's summer, then I can guarantee you we are outside on my sweet balcony, feeling the ocean breeze kiss our skin as we converse. Either way, we are present with one another because stories are when, as Anne Lamott writes, "Something happened you didn't expect, that led to some deep internal change in yourself or the main character. Tell it."[2]

---

[2] Lamott, Anne. *Almost Everything*. Riverhead Books, 2018.

CHAPTER 2

Parents

> "Parents can only give good advice or put them on the right path, but the final form of a person's character lies in their own hands."
> –Anne Frank

As a daughter to my beloved parents and two of my life's best teachers, figuratively, not literally, I was the firstborn. And with that came expectations. I would learn much about these, and they would serve me well. They would also be the hurdles that I would need to climb over or even knock over and push to the sidelines.

Being the first of four daughters was a challenging space to occupy.

As a high school English teacher, one of the first questions I am asked when I fill out college recommendations for students is, "What are the first few adjectives that come to you when you think of this applicant?" If I were filling that application out for me as a teen applicant, I would select the words responsible, leader, organized, and poised. Of course, these words change and develop over time, but most of my life, while growing up, I felt like I was at the helm of a large ship in a constant position of responsibility.

It was not easy. It was rarely fun. Fun was typically earned.

I grew up in the beautiful city of San Clemente—the Spanish village by the sea. Proudly displayed in its architecture, its popular beaches promote a lifestyle of famous surfing and sunsets. It is a city that boasts "World's Best Climate" as we soak up about 300 days of sunshine and live in an average temperature of 73 degrees.

My dad was a successful, self-employed, union plumbing contractor by trade. He also was a great saver. He knew how to save money to make dreams happen, and many of them did as a result of his vision and hard work. He taught me the value of having what he called "a rat hole." It was his method of earning extra money and putting it aside. He exemplified consistency as he would wake up every morning at 5:20, make his coffee and English muffin, read the newspaper, prepare his lunch box for the day, and then get dressed in his heavy-duty jeans and construction boots. He never complained. Never. He would come home at the end of his day, his hands rough and calloused from fitting pipes, with dirt and mud on his clothes, and then shower and shave to meet us for dinner every night as a family at our dining room table. It was a routine that mattered. Even though, with four young girls, we had lots of spilled milk. Lots!

He came from a large Catholic family in New York with seven siblings all together! It was a house filled with loud memories. My dad loved family, football, and cars and learned how to fix almost everything, minus items that had to do with electricity! Anytime something required electrical knowledge, we all took to the hills. His frustration came to a head in this area, and patience was not his strong suit—nor is it mine. But, other than that, he was truly my hero. He still is. So much stands out to me about him that makes him shine.

On Valentine's Day, for example, single, divorced, or married, my dad would bring us each a box of See's chocolates and a hand-written card. The card sometimes had misspelled words because my dad learned to spell phonetically. My mom used to try to fix the cards or even write them, but later, I shared that I loved the errors as they were perfectly imperfect reflections of my dad. I saved those cards and have some of them right now on my refrigerator. He also saved up for a boat. Unbeknownst to us, he was working side jobs and stashing money aside in his "rat hole" for his dream—a ski boat. One day, he pulled his plumbing truck into the driveway with this wonderful boat in tow for our family. Used, but paid for by my dad's extra hard work so we could go on water-skiing trips and make memories that lasted a lifetime.

My parents both worked to provide creative and affordable ways to get away as a family and have fun. When I was in the fourth grade, they bought our first motorhome. It was a dream they wanted to fulfill, and they did. So we had a motorhome and a boat in tow. The memories are priceless, and the efforts toward building a family of my parents are unmatched.

My mom was a stay-at-home mom with many responsibilities to keep the home running. She also ran her own home business as a child-care provider and part-time typist. Coming from a home where she was an only child, I don't know how she managed, but she did, and she was a woman of great order. She was a mom of great order and admired by many. Daily, parents would bring their children into her care while they went off to their given careers. My mom was the one who kept those children safe and cared for and filled them with both play and order. What a ministry she led for 25 years. She still made time to take us to the park and the library, to read biographies, and to teach us how to be workers at home, and she served as a Girl Scout leader for us and many other girls, providing opportunities that many would only wish for.

She also taught me how to overcome. Specifically, when I was an 8th-grade student, I was assigned to read a book on Thomas Edison and then write a report. At the time, this particular science teacher disliked me; at least, that was my perception. So, my mom, in her wisdom, instructed me to handwrite the entire report and then type the finished paper. Next, my mom had me attach the handwritten report to the final report. It was my mom's way of helping me prove that it was all my work. It seemed daunting, but I did it. The end result was an A+. I still have that report! And I learned that our character is often tested, and we need to take steps of integrity to bring it out into the open when it is perhaps discounted or maybe misunderstood. It also helped me in my career as a teacher. I work with diligence to help my students feel understood.

My mom also helped me become a public speaker. She would make me stand in our backyard with my 3x5 index cards, speech in hand, and proclaim why I should be ASB president. Over and over. I won. This was another stepping stone to my work as a teacher and speaker. I am forever grateful. On her desk sat a sign "Wonder-Woman Works Here." She was.

On top of all the responsibilities my parents shouldered, with no family around to help, I was diagnosed with a rare form of cancer as a six-month-old infant—Retinoblastoma. Not a trace of it in my family. For the reader not well-versed in the disease, this is a rare type of eye cancer that develops in the retina and can occur in one or both eyes. Fortunately for me, it was only my right eye. It has few, if any, symptoms at first. My mom just happened to notice that my right eye was not tracking exactly as my left when she was feeding me. That, in and of itself, is miraculous, as it is malignant. Even the ophthalmologist did not see it upon my first visit. It was as my mom was preparing to leave his office that he said if she wanted to be sure I was alright, she could schedule a visit in two weeks for my eye to be dilated.

Two weeks later, my eyes were dilated, and the mass was visible. Shortly thereafter, surgery was performed at UCSF, and then followed a very new, unexpected path of life for my parents.

While I do not remember any of those early years, I do remember the stares and the questions from complete strangers. Not a day went by that I was not asked, "What's wrong with your eye?" And the staring of people, adults and children alike, was so obvious. I felt like an anomaly, a strange being, like the *Ugly Duckling* by Danish poet and author Hans Christian Andersen. What was clear to the onlooker was my prosthetic eye. It did look different. It was different. I was different. I could do everything a "normal" child could do, and I compensated well by learning to just turn my head to see on my right side, but it wasn't until more improved ocular prosthetics and implants were made that I had the opportunity to improve my appearance.

As the years went on and my parents wisely enrolled me in school, life felt normal. Once I was able to tell my story, and after the kids freaked out a bit, I felt accepted. It was the rest of the world, that which was not insulated, that made it so hard. The interesting take on this is that, for me, having a handicap (no vision in my right eye, an artificial eye) did not feel like a handicap. I was able to adjust and really had no idea what it was like to have dual vision. I'm thankful for this. Really, the only way it is a handicap is that my vision is blocked on my right, so I can miss some great opportunities on the pickleball court or wack my head if I am not using my left eye and rotating my head completely to see what is on my right! I have had doctors and psychologists say that this is a traumatic event with many rippling effects on me. I have even had well-meaning friends pray that I would be "healed." And while this trauma may be true, and having an artificial eye may be life-altering today, I do not feel this. I learned to overcome one episode at a time and to understand that my life is full of hope, healing, and purpose. It has really never prevented me from doing anything I wanted to do.

My three sisters and I were educated in a local Catholic school, and Sunday mass was a regular part of our week. Our family friends were Catholic, and we were well-versed in Catechism and the sacraments of the Catholic church. My best friends came from school and church, but the classroom memories were not necessarily my favorite memories.

At the time and in that place, fear and shame were acceptable means of teaching and school discipline. The imprints left on my young mind hurt like an eyelash in my eye. In fifth grade, I can still see the class point system that was permanently on the board, listing the homework and conduct grades of every student for all to see. My conduct was always high. My homework? Not so high. I averaged 70% and often saw below it. So did the rest of my class. It felt like a board of shame. It was a constant visual of how dumb I felt academically. When teachers at the school were mean, really mean, I'd just allow the stamp of "stupid" to stay engraved on my forehead.

I didn't understand that this Catholic school was presenting me with a false representation of who I was and who I would become. My definition of God came from these well-meaning, devoted people, and yet, they were often so very harsh. They taught with a foundation of fear, not of care or love. Their definition of love, I would learn later, was not mine. Perhaps the philosophy and theology of teaching at the time had zero to do with a love of learning but a fear of learning or else. It was so confusing as these were people who gave their lives to the Catholic church. Some were nuns or priests, and others were lay teachers who taught me about God.

I learned how to avoid disappointing them. Performance was the answer.

From first grade through eighth, I stayed in that school setting. I made great memories and had lots of opportunities. I played guitar in church, received my first holy communion, and had my first crush. I grew friendships with roots that developed because we were able to stay in the same school. This was truly good. I still have connections with some of these wonderful former students today.

After-school hours were anger-producing. Being the oldest daughter was a constant chore. My mom depended on me, and my role as the oldest sister came with an exhausting amount of household work. My sisters and I still talk about the mounds and mounds of folding we did, the dishes we washed, the cleaning we performed, and the perfection that was expected. Sitting in our family room, my mom would bring in basket after basket of clean clothes that needed to be folded and put away. It felt never-ending. Other responsibilities included (as most kids do) dishes, emptying the dishwasher, cleaning the house every Saturday, and then doing outside chores with my dad. We were so relieved when he finally hired a gardener. My parents wanted us to be responsible and, to their credit, we are. Each of us is extremely responsible. Yet, many times, this felt so unfair. It left room for play only when all else was accomplished. Life felt like one huge responsibility with little to no room for fun.

Fear as a daughter or as a son can linger for years. As a child, it is normal to have a sense of healthy fear like an apprehension or as in profound reverence. It's natural when it alerts us to something that may be wrong or dangerous.

Like walking alongside a railroad track and hearing the train. It is the body's primal response to a threat.

According to Dr. Christine Celio, Ph.D, in her article "Fear can be good—in small doses,"[3] "It usually causes a physical response in which the brain activates the body's sympathetic nervous system. You may know this as a 'fight or flight' response. When the sympathetic nervous system engages, our bodies undergo several physical changes:

- → Epinephrine and other stress hormones flood your system
- → Your heart starts pounding
- → Breathing becomes fast and shallow
- → Your pupils dilate to better assess exit routes
- → Digestion slows down
- → Your bladder relaxes

"What's interesting," Celio continues, "about the physical fear response is that one person may find it energizing and heady, while another person may find it unnerving and uncomfortable."[4]

Fear served a purpose for me growing up. It motivated me to meet my parents' expectations. I saw them as God's agents. I saw them as my Higher Power(s). My first

---

[3] https://www.drchristinecelio.com/
[4] https://www.onemedical.com/blog/healthy-living/what-is-fear/

representatives of a Higher Power. This has its appropriate place. It is good, for a time.

My mom and dad symbolize this differently. My mom was the one in charge. My dad was the one who worked outside of the home and came home each night knowing my mom had the house and his girls taken care of. In the 1970s, moms were typically the disciplinarians, and dads worked outside the home as the primary source of income. Children were expected to be responsible for things such as homework and chores. When adults instructed us to be home by curfew (or there would be consequences), we came home on time. Holding us accountable and having the fear of God instilled in us, the fear of authority contributes to how we turn out as adults. It has its pros and cons.

How did my parents serve, in my eyes, as Higher Powers? What was that, exactly? Well, it was me knowing that they were in charge. What they said was the ultimate voice of authority. While I understand that much of this is just a part of good parenting, it lacked a role for me as I developed into a young woman trying to exercise her sense of self. I did not know who I was; I only really knew how to be the daughter my parents wanted me to be for them. The fear I felt when I tried to speak in disagreement or challenge my mom was met with consequences. What was important to me was often discounted and trumped by my mom's demands. I grew to just fall in line like a military cadet. It was easier that way.

While I know that her role needed me to fall in line to some degree, it felt stifling and caused me to not speak honestly about what was important to me or my sense of self. This pressed in on me like an iron on an ironing board working out the wrinkles on a clean cotton shirt. It felt heavy, and while it did iron me out to my parents' expectations, it scorched my heart and sometimes my confidence.

Was that good for me as I moved forward as a teen and then adult? For me, it became an unhealthy fear because there was no clear directive from it. Rather than inspiring me to take action that would be good for me, it left me feeling defenseless. I felt doubtful. I could not make the decisions I wanted to make and be okay without having approval. I was afraid to make a mistake. Because, for me, that approval was equated with love. If I met with approval, I was praised. So, I tried very hard to meet that approval.

I could not reconcile how to be a young woman of faith and a young woman who could trust in a God I was supposed to follow. I knew rules and religion but was afraid that if I made too many mistakes, I'd be punished badly by God. I was not at all sure that God loved me. If He did, it was because I performed well. I often felt the same way with my parents; if I performed well, I was accepted. I don't remember feeling connected by love because I was just Lynn, their daughter. It felt tied to what I did. It was my perspective as a young adult.

I also thought, at times, that if I made my parents angry enough or didn't live the way they expected me to live, I'd be a disappointment to them. And to God.

But then there were moments where I understood their love. Like the time when my mom took the time to explain to me through slides and literature what an abortion was, and after I took it all in as best I could as a teen, she said, "Nothing you could ever do would cause me to not love you." I knew it. I knew she meant it. I knew she loved me.

My vision of a Higher Power was founded on my parents and the Catholic experience. It was, at the time, fear-based and works-based. I have met many people who experienced the same. I have also met many who greatly revere it.

So my initiation into a HP began with, like most all of us, my parents and the religion we practiced growing up.

Many episodes took place where my mom, particularly, was my HP. She was a woman I feared, and saying "no" to her was never an option. This caused me to have both a fear of her and respect for her until I learned differently. Fortunately, because of my 12-step work, I understand this to be very different. Today, I respect her. I revere her. I recognize her work as a woman and mother.

Years later, I have a very different understanding of how she loved me and how my dad made meaning of his role as her husband (it was not easy, but it was how it worked for them), and it is okay. They showed me their love the way they knew best—based on their experiences. We don't know what we don't know. And, more importantly, we are people who are trying to extract meaning from our worldview, which usually begins with our parents' worldview.

After EMDR therapy, I learned that they, like me, are products of what they learned. When people say, "They did the best they knew how." I really do understand this. Additionally, I see that my parents created in me the many strengths that I have and value today. Even as of late, with my parents in their late 80s, I know that the voice I so desperately wanted to have is now the voice I later developed and I now have for my parents. It is a voice of love and protection.

I also see my character defects. I work to shed these, but anger is not an emotion harbored in the way my dear mom and dad raised me. It is not a fault-finding way of life for me. I am not a victim. It is a gratitude-filled way of life, most of the time, with grace and understanding. It is an opportunity for me to use, as one author, Anne Lamott, shares, "Spiritual WD40," with a skinny straw that can be sprayed in all the nooks and crannies. They were my Higher Powers for a long time until I was ready to expand and change that story, learn a different one, and choose a different one.

My sweet, hard-working parents married in 1960. Today, they are pillars of commitment. As I write this, they are probably nested in their easy, remote-controlled chairs with their favorite television show, "Jeopardy," on, and they are most likely enjoying a hot dinner simply and sweetly. Theirs is a relationship filled with ease and grace. They are life companions who love and care deeply for one another. I see this and know that my parents have endured many of life's blessings and hardships. They do it well together.

CHAPTER 3

Sisters

"A sister is a little bit of childhood that can never be lost."
–Marion Garretty

"If you don't understand how a woman could both love her sister dearly and want to wring her neck at the same time, then you were probably an only child."
–Linda Sunshine

I love my four sisters. We are also radically different from one another. I am the oldest and considered the responsible one, the decision maker, the teacher. Kendall is next and is the detailed, committed to serving, event coordinator extraordinaire, sensitive one. She is the Martha in our family. Brynn is the hostess with the mostest, the frugal one, and the one who questions and weighs her decisions carefully until she eventually makes them. She is like a compass that ponders true North with an ever-moving needle. Mae is the center-stage sister who feeds on being in the limelight and lives to love and laugh. She is big on relationships, fun, and drama.

Growing up in a family of four girls was a bit crazy. Actually, it was often crazy. We shared rooms so that Kendall and I were in one room, and Brynn and Mae were in another. It made for lots of baby dolls, Barbies, and bustling bedrooms. It led to some wild teenage weekends and facilitated frequent clothes-stealing with excessive squabbling.

Watching the film *Little Women* (2019) reminds me of sisterhood and the heartfelt moments smothered sometimes by anger and possessiveness. It is a timeless tale that, like my own story of growing up with three sisters, is filled with affection, anger, and empathy, as well as love and sensibility to our various roles as sisters. We are different and captivating in our own way.

I was deemed the one in charge of all three of my sisters. I was the leader, the decision-maker, and the babysitter. It was a horrible, unwanted, unpaid position, and I felt it terribly unfair. I did not know how to manage them as a sister just two or a few years older, yet it was expected.

For example, I can remember being left in the car with them after Sunday mass and having to wait for my parents as they went motor home shopping. I would be left in the car as the babysitter. As soon as my two youngest sisters saw my mom and dad step away from the car and I was in charge, they would act uncontrollably crazy. It was like trying to tie up two wild horses in a coral. I would beg them, bribe them, and even cry. They would only laugh and carry on further. We'd be promised lunch at McDonald's if we were "good," but I could not manage them, and it was a terrible time for me. Their behavior was tied to my reward or remuneration. I felt powerless because I was.

The expectation of being the responsible older sister was huge, and while I understand now that it was likely how my parents thought it should be because it would teach me responsibility, it felt like a suitcase I was unable to lift and carry. Being held responsible for my siblings at my expense was heavy, and a role I would later learn became the seedlings for codependency.

Responsibility is a Higher Power for many people. It is tied to value. How? Because for me, as I took on this expected role for my sisters and made sure that what needed to get done got done, rewards followed. So, I worked hard to be that sister. If I aimed high and showed up as responsible, I was rewarded. I gained privileges, and these privileges meant freedom. Freedom from the responsibility monster. Or so I thought. Little did I know the monster would be attached to me like a dog on a leash. The dog thinks it is free but quickly finds out that he's not; the leash has him in the hands of his master.

Today, we all live within a thirty-minute drive of one another. We used to have family gatherings around Christmas and sometimes birthdays, and there were times that we did a bit of vacationing together. Previously, we celebrated life events together and yet respected our individual family lives. I can now accept each sister for who she is, and it comes with grace and lots of surrender. It is an opportunity for me to practice and pray.

One author who has helped me understand this idea is Byron Katie. If you struggle with accepting people as they are, I highly recommend her work. It is literally called "The Work."[5] She says, "I am a lover of what is, not because I'm a spiritual person, but because it hurts when we argue with reality." I totally get this. It's not my favorite practice, but I am working on it.

The responsibility for my sisters is a thing of the past. Being in fear of them is also an issue of the past. It no longer has a connection to my relationship with them. Being the responsible older sister is no longer how I define myself in our family, with the exception of my parents.

New to me is how to weave my role as a sister among the four of us as we care for my aging parents. Each brings different definitions and ideas of how to do this. It is one where one sister wants to have an action plan NOW, another wants to hire help yesterday, another is a sort of anxious

---

[5] https://thework.com/

mother bear, and then me … wanting to consider it all and then present options to my parents for them to decide unless it becomes clear they cannot decide for themselves.

It's another opportunity for me to see that I need a Higher Power, and it is not my sisters. This is new territory. I do know that I need to listen to my sisters, taking into account their individual experiences and love for my parents as we allow life to unfold and take the next indicated steps. It requires, for me, the willingness to understand the fear that is involved in these decisions for my parents and the fear we each feel as we consider what might be the next best course of action. I am also reminded in that same breath that "perfect love casts out fear."[6] And that kind of love comes from God.

Being the oldest sister requires me to seek outside counsel. This has proved to be invaluable and has required a willingness to hear that more needs to be considered. To seek what is best for my parents and to keep my heart and mind open to their needs and wishes as we take the next steps for their lives. I do my absolute best to honor my parents and respect what they want and need. I also know that this is a biblical command. Here is a story that will likely fine-tune the reason my sisters are no longer my HPs, nor am I in any fear of them.

In the summer of 2022, my parents realized that they needed to revise their family trust. It became very messy and complicated beyond my imagination.

---

[6] 1 John 4:18

Let me explain.

In 2011, when I filed for my divorce from my husband of 26 years, two huge consequences came. One was my two oldest children deciding to never speak to me again. The second was my parents removing me from their trust as their trustee and naming my ex-husband to take my place. I will spare the reader the emotional anguish that this brought me, but suffice it to say that it was unbelievable and certainly heartbreaking.

The rippling effects of divorce are horrible, and many people wrongly make judgments. It is unnecessary, unhelpful, and unkind. Why? Because they have no idea what it is like to be in that marriage under those particular circumstances. No idea. Furthermore, they are not God. He is All-Knowing, not those who often cast stones. I have learned so much about this from my own family and friends and my students.

Fast-forward two years from my divorce, and my younger two daughters and I connected and reestablished our relationship in a tenuous manner. This was understandable, so I worked very hard to gain them back into my life.

My parents gradually saw my ex-husband for who he is and, as a result, distanced themselves from him. This allowed me to rebuild a healthy relationship with them. I did not expect them to understand the magnitude of my decision to divorce, but I did hope and pray that they would accept me and my decision without judgment. It took a long time for us to move forward, but eventually, we did.

In July of 2022, Danny (my husband) and I were out of the country on vacation, and my parents contacted me. They asked me if I would serve as their trustee along with my brother-in-law and if I would help them procure an attorney to make this change and a few other amendments to their trust. By this time, I had been sober from alcohol for five years, and I believe that my life of service and integrity stood out to them in new and profound ways. Additionally, I possess skills and experience that suit well for leadership.

The bad news is that I made a terrible mistake about a year before this took place. I had asked my parents for a ring that was my mom's original engagement ring. It held sentimental value to me rather than being an item of great material worth (approximately $2,300). Upon hearing my request and its reasoning, my parents immediately gave me the ring. The problem arose because my mom had designated it in the trust to my nephew. This caused a HUGE problem among my three sisters. Following a Zoom meeting with my sisters, during which they expressed their fury and attack, I understood the situation from their perspective, and I asked their forgiveness. The next day, my husband met my parents and returned the ring to them. He asked that they not discuss it with me as it was not needed; the ring was a source of discord. I wanted none of that and wanted to return it to them so that any animosity and mistrust would stop.

I never intended to take the ring from my nephew. However, one of my sisters accused me of "stealing" the ring from her family. While this is her perspective, it is not mine. I did not have any malicious intent, but it was presumed and believed by all three of my sisters. They built a belief system that led to discord and hate. And my asking forgivness did not seem to matter.

A few weeks later, my parents called me, wanting to know the full story. Reluctantly, I disclosed everything to them. They thanked me and said they would decide, and it would go into the trust along with their other many designated items. Additionally, my dad revealed that he had previously given my niece several items of jewelry that she had expressed interest in, but this was not disclosed by her mother, my sister. He explained that he and my mom could do whatever they wanted with their possessions; it was their prerogative. I agreed.

During the attorney's process of drafting my parents' trust, they requested my presence at the appointment. My sisters were clearly upset as they wanted to be involved and wished for the meeting to be recorded. They contacted me, asking me to record the meeting. I explained that it was not my decision and that they would need to ask my parents as it was their meeting and business. On the morning of their meeting, my sister called my mom, and she and my dad agreed to the recording.

The meeting took place, and the attorney recorded it on my mom's phone. While the conversation proceeded, I was simply present. I did not interject my opinion on anything. When the attorney inquired about new or specific changes, my parents informed him, and one change, unknown to me at the time, was to designate me as the recipient of the ring. The meeting continued, and I remained silent. My dad made the statement to me that he paid close attention to the fact that while they had designated $25,000 to each of their six grandchildren, my four children would not be a part of their inheritance, and I said nothing to intervene as I respect their wishes and know it is for their reasons. It is their financial portfolio, not mine. It also is subject to change anytime they decide to change it.

After listening to the recorded meeting and learning about the decision regarding the ring, my sisters banded together and stated that I should have said something to prevent the ring from being given to me. They questioned why I didn't speak up, emphasizing that I was supposed to "protect" my mom's original plan for the ring to go to my nephew. "What is more important, the ring or the relationship with my sisters and the entire family?" My three sisters escalated this issue to our extended family, including nieces, nephews, and my children. They conveyed that "they are all aware of what you (Lynn) have done." Subsequently, I received a threatening text from my sisters stating that my response would "affect how we will proceed in the future."

My sisters, shortly thereafter, requested a meeting. My parents declined. They had no reason to have a meeting. They asked me to help them write a text message to respond to my sisters' request. Given their limited comfort with technology, I sat with them and composed the message verbatim as they dictated it. Every word of it was from them. Once completed, I then copied and pasted it to my mom's cell phone, and she sent it. My dad hugged me and then kissed me as I left them that day. He thanked me for helping them.

It is clear that I am to honor my parents. I do not serve my sisters, nor am I in fear of them or their narrative. Psalm 29:25: "Fear of man will prove to be a snare, but whoever trusts in the Lord will be kept safe." I am very sad about the pain, and I sought wise counsel over this for several months. One woman, a CPA who experienced very similar family trust issues, made the following statements to me:

1. My parents are under no obligation to tell anyone what they are potentially giving.
2. Live like my parents are giving it all away to their favorite charity.

3. All their money needs to be saved under the trust because it may all be needed for the long-term care of my parents.
4. I am a daughter to my parents first.
5. I am to seek God's approval ahead of all others.

My next steps proceeded what took place next, including much prayer, self-reflection, work, and wise counsel. In August 2022, my sisters emailed the first of many ugly emails. They had banded together against me and my parents. They insisted on each having a copy of my parent's trust.

I prayed and read many verses in my Bible to help me. I was seeking the help of a Higher Power. "I am the God who heals."[7] And, "Therefore, as God's chosen people, holy and dearly loved, clothe yourselves with compassion, kindness, humility, gentleness and patience. Bear with each other and forgive one another if any of you has a grievance against someone. Forgive as the Lord forgave you. And over all these virtues put on love, which binds them all together in perfect unity."[8] Ok, I thought. Maybe these Bible verses will help me.

On October 7, 2022, we planned a family meeting at my parent's home. I went willing to listen and be open to whatever God would have me do or say. What came out was hate, bitterness, and resentment from my sister, Brynn. She

---

[7] James 4:2
[8] Colossians 3:12–14

is truly the "accuser of the brethren." From Kendall came a reserved willingness to move toward trust and forgiveness. She was clearly hurt by my action to ask my parents for the ring. I understood and asked for forgiveness wholeheartedly from all of them again for any pain that I caused. Mae was a source to be reckoned with. She disrespected my dad repeatedly by insisting that they each receive a copy of the trust even though their attorney had written them all saying that they would not be receiving a copy. Each time I spoke up for my parents' wishes, I was attacked. At one point, my dad said, "Stop attacking Lynn." Every time he said, "No, you will not get copies of the trust until we die," Mae would say, "Stop" to my dad. She claimed that "transparency" was the solution to all this. My dad said no. At one point, my dad asked me what I thought. I said that I think he and my mom should follow the advice of their attorney. Mae added, "Do not ask Lynn. Do not ask David "(the attorney). She absolutely disrespects authority and my parents' wishes. I felt sick. I left their home knowing that I went with the willingness to seek unity and honor my parents. I was faithful to that and that I had asked my sisters for forgiveness.

In October 2022, the attorney sent a letter to my three sisters stating that my parents requested his assistance in addressing the issues that had arisen from their estate process. He made it clear that the trust is my parents and theirs alone. He stated that nothing was hidden, and it provides equal distribution to each daughter. It is a fair disposition of their estate after they pass. "Nobody has exerted any influence over their decisions," and, essentially, they can do whatever they want at any time. He closed by requesting they discontinue asking for copies of the estate plan documents and asked for their cooperation.

On November 14, 2022, my sisters taped a letter to my parents' front door. My mom called me at work to tell me. She did not know what to do. It basically stated that they would not be continuing a relationship with my parents.

Again, my parents asked me to contact the attorney, and we emailed him the letter from my sisters. He expressed his "shock" and sorrow for my parents and me for having to "put up with this." It was sad, but he agreed that he was on our team and would figure out a way to address this. He did. He wrote a three-page letter and was clear to add that the three sisters understand that the correspondence with our parents, the demands to be a part of that process, and leveraging an ongoing relationship on being looped into their planning process border on elderly abuse. He would make it a legal matter if necessary. He closed by asking them to focus on re-engaging with my parents and in a productive manner as parents and children.

Thanksgiving was different. My sisters did not include my parents or me. So, I invited my parents to join me at my husband's family home. It was lovely and loving.

Christmas was just around the corner, and the pain of not being together for my parents was real and hurtful. My dad told me of his hurt. I felt sick for him and my mom.

The next thing I knew, my mom and dad sent a group text message to all of us saying that whatever they did, please forgive them and that they wanted to celebrate Christmas. My sisters said they "forgave" them. I was baffled but understood that my parents did not want to miss a family Christmas. So, we all showed up at my parents' home a few days before Christmas and had the traditional meal and time around the tree. It was okay, and I went with the understanding that I was to be helpful and caring. I would honor my parents and show kindness to my sisters.

Following the Christmas event, I invested time with my parents and continue to do so. The series of events that followed were just emails. They became increasingly cold and challenging. So, this has led to my need to seek emotional sobriety and to understand the very real and ugly parts of my family.

For example, in April of 2023, my sister Brynn decided to host Easter. It has been our family tradition to celebrate this and most major holidays as a family. This time was very different. She included my parents but not me. Instead, she invited my ex-husband and my children and granddaughter. My ex-husband told me on the phone that week that this was new—that his ex-sister-in-law was reaching out. Hmmm, I thought. My sister claimed that she now wants to alternate certain holidays between me and my ex-husband. It has been 12 years! Suddenly, she has a heart for him with no conversation with me about this. Incidentally, she reneged her claim and has not included me even though she told me and my parents she would. The truth is clear on her intentions.

When I called my ex-husband, he commented that it had only been in the past 12 months that my sister, Brynn, started reaching out. In addition, my two daughters, whom I have built a relationship with over the years since my divorce, now want "space" between me and them. It is so incredibly sad to see this unfold before me. When I sought counsel from my therapist, she advised me to contact my daughter in Texas and let her know that I love her and want to fly to her state to see her and talk with her about whatever she needs to know—to shed light on possible darkness. I contacted her, but she was not interested. She said in a follow-up text that she wanted space and would reach out to me when she was ready. I simply responded with, "Ok, honey."

In June 2023, I went to the mailbox. In it was a typed letter from my daughter in Texas.

Before opening it, I had a conversation with God. I thanked Him for the letter no matter what it contained. I reminded myself that I already turned my will and life over to His care. I reminded myself that I am His child, that He is there for me, and that I am loved by Him and nothing happens to me that He and I cannot walk through together—big sigh. I released the content of the letter to Him.

It read:

Mom,

I wanted to reach out to you about my upcoming wedding. After careful consideration and reflection on our relationship, I have made the difficult decision not to invite you to the wedding.

This decision was not easy for me, and I understand that it may be hurtful for you to hear. Please know that it is in no way a reflection of our bond or the love I have for you as my mom. It is based on personal circumstances and a desire for the day to be as peaceful and joyful as possible.

I believe that it is important for both of us to be honest and open about our feelings, and I genuinely hope that you can find it in your heart to respect my choice. I value our relationship and trust that we can find a way to move forward despite this decision.

Sincerely,
Your Daughter

Part of me hesitates to reveal all of this. I do not want to create a picture of victimization, as that is not the case. It is my reality. And reality is just that, reality, 100% of the time. When I sought my sponsor's thoughts on this part of my story, she said, as did my husband and other wise individuals, that it could help others. They said it could show how I gained freedom and strength by shifting my focus from my sisters and family to a very different Higher Power. I sincerely hope it does serve this purpose because writing it is more painful than I care to admit. I often cannot believe this is my life. But it is, and it is shaping me spiritually in ways I had never thought possible.

I've never felt closer to God nor trusted in Him like I do now. Like the woman who was healed by Jesus in the New Testament, who believed that touching the edge of his cloak would heal her, I've attached myself to God through my experiences with my sisters and children. She said to herself, "If only I touch his cloak, I will be healed." When Jesus turned and saw her, he said, "Take heart daughter, your faith has healed you."[9] A church pastor taught that the word "touched" means that she attached herself to his cloak. I love that image. Because of my sisters and my children, He is my Higher Power, regardless of how people behave. It's both beautiful and liberating for me.

---

[9] Matthew 9:21–22

Through all of this, God revealed to me how to lead a purposeful life and be emotionally independent from the expectations or fear of others.

The day of my daughter's wedding came and went with my parents respectfully declining their invitation in support of my decision while I embraced the companionship of my new "family." The only way I can describe how I felt that day was loved. I was surrounded by love. I felt grace, peace, and a sense of purpose. It was a beautiful November day in Southern California with glorious sun, and I am sure my daughter looked beautiful, and her husband was beaming, but while many guests and my sisters were in attendance, the absence of my daughter's mother was genuinely heartbreaking.

CHAPTER 4

Wife

The long chapter because being married for 26 years is a l-o-n-g time.

"I, ____, take thee, ____, to be my wedded husband/wife, to have and to hold, from this day forward, for better, for worse, for richer, for poorer, in sickness and in health, to love and to cherish, till death do us part, according to God's holy ordinance; and thereto I pledge thee my faith [or] pledge myself to you." –theknot.com

Snow White. Sleeping Beauty. Cinderella. Yes, the last one, Cinderella. That's me. She is the one I most identify with. Once upon a time, there was a young, beautiful girl named Lynn. She lived with her mom, dad, and three sisters. They were not mean like Cinderella's stepmother or stepsisters, but she did do a lot of work to be responsible and to be accepted. Lynn tried her best to make her mom and dad happy. She attended school, worked hard to get good enough grades, had lots of friends, played a musical instrument, and was skilled in cooking, cleaning, and caring for others. She even went to church, where she learned more about what a woman needed to be for a man. She received a lot of attention from potential suitors and went on many dates.

In high school, I met an exceptional young man. We met at an ice cream store where I worked part-time. From the moment I saw him, I remember an immediate attraction. I felt nervous just seeing him walk into the store. A few days later, he drove past my house. I felt shocked and then super nervous as he saw me in the driveway while he drove past and then backed up his car! We talked briefly, and I learned he lived just down the street! The next thing I remember, we were putting cards on one another's cars and then met up at a school dance. He asked me to dance, and that night was one I will always remember. I did not want the night to end. We sat on the curb of our high school parking lot, and I felt like I wanted to be next to him for as long as possible. The chemistry was strong, and our interests in life, as we knew them then, were well-matched.

While he was at work one day, I asked him to the winter formal dance via a card I left on his car. I still remember the card. It had a spigot on the front, and it poured out a rainbow. I was so nervous about what he would think or how he'd respond. It was apparently an easy "yes" on his part, but it sure gave me a sensitivity to what anticipated rejection can feel like.

We became a couple after that dance. And we "danced" through the rest of high school together. We even continued on to junior college together, taking classes that would allow us to be together as often as possible. We were a couple that everyone knew as just that, a couple. Maybe that sounds silly, but it was pretty rare to be as connected as we were and committed to each other at that stage of our young lives.

He was the first guy I chose to be intimate with, and, at that time, I felt entirely comfortable with that choice. I had thought long and hard about it, done my research, sought my gynecologist to seek birth control, and knew that if I were to get pregnant, I would marry him. Despite being just 17, I felt responsible for my decisions. He took my breath away, and we knew that we were committed to one another because we loved each other. I can say that it felt unquestionably right.

Had we given ourselves more time to mature, and had I listened to my inner self, we might have married. I have no doubt about that. I didn't. He was all in, and I know it must have been baffling to him to see me leave for a four-year college after we'd been together for so long, but I did. And I made the horrible decision to break up before college and date other men. I regret the pain I caused us both and the life we might have made together. I know it would have been really good. He was a wonderful man who worked hard to be the outstanding man he is today.

If I had not been so young and inexperienced, I might have known that we were quite possibly a divine match. But, once again, I made the "everybodies" in my life the influencers. The Higher Powers.

My mom made it clear that since he wasn't college-educated (planning to be a firefighter and later a deputy chief), he would not be a marriage candidate. She was very sure that a college graduate was the ticket for my future security. I assumed and trusted that she was right, even though it felt so wrong. Years later, forty to be exact, she shared that she was wrong. She knew he was a good man and would have made a great husband and father. It felt so comforting to hear, like the ending of a story you wait to hear.

During my early 20s, I found part-time work in a grocery store. Actually, I had many jobs as a teen, but this was the last one I would have before going off to college. One day, while working, I met a man who was five years older and an employee of the store. He was finishing graduate school and lived on his own. He was financially secure. He was very quiet and reserved. He was responsible. He cared about and for his mother. After all, she was a widow, and he was, like me, the responsible older son. I became interested. He seemed to spell security.

This same feeling was not the case at his mother's. The television was on, the house looked like a museum, and the carpet looked like it had never been walked on. I thought to myself, do I take my shoes off? I had on a pretty dress and was unsure if I should remove my heels or leave them on. As I came near, I could tell this would be an unusual meeting, a cold meeting. Even his body language became tightened, just like hers. I should have taken serious mental notes as this was telling me something. But, my enthusiastic, optimistic personality took over the truth. I even thought, "It doesn't matter. I'm not dating her; I'm dating him." This, I now know, was my excuse for what was true. I was entering a family of emotionally disconnected people.

The conversation and evening were polite. I embraced the unembraceable woman. I believed I could overcome this and come out shining.

I want to emphasize something I learned much later: When we marry, we marry the family. It may be from a distance, but it has residual effects. Do not underestimate this. It may work for you, but be very careful and honest in your assessment. Do not deny the truth. When people tell you who they are, believe them. I hope you understand my message here.

In fact, at one point, after we became engaged, I wrote his mother a letter—a heart-felt letter titled "Daughter-in-love." As a mother of only sons, it was my attempt to write her as her first "daughter" and thank her for raising the man I was about to marry. I wanted to build a bridge toward her regardless of our personality differences. I wanted to honor her as his mother and my future mother-in-law. It took me quite a while to compose it. Since my number one love language is words, it mattered—every word was carefully considered. I felt so good when I mailed it to her. To my bewilderment, she never acknowledged its contents, only that she had received it. It was like putting a bucket into a well and letting it go deep only to retrieve it with no water inside—empty. For her, this was normal. I would find this to be true over and over again as the future unfolded. Her critical spirit and relationship with her son were ugly from my perspective. It was based on how well her financial portfolio was and how he managed it. Performance-based acceptance was the relationship they shared and understood. She was his Higher Power.

Later, as the relationship developed, I learned that his father was an alcoholic. When he died in his early fifties, he left his wife with plenty of financial resources but little knowledge of how to manage those resources. Guess who came to the rescue? Yes, my then-husband did. His two other brothers were of no help. One was in Alaska, hiding. The other was a perpetual playboy who was allergic to all things responsible. He, like his deceased father, was also an alcoholic. While this care-taking was admirable at the onset, it led to an unhealthy pattern that did not make room for healthy leaving and cleaving.

All this should have been loud and clear to me. Sadly, naively, it wasn't. I only saw what I wanted to see. I saw, as my own mom saw and taught me, education and financial security were the keys to my future. They were, however, not the keys to my heart or wholeness. Nor my heart that desired to be known and loved.

Since he was well-educated (he earned a college and master's degree) and hard-working, I would have the power to turn him into the fabulous and loving man I dreamed of marrying. The foundation was set, and I believed it would provide security. I felt overjoyed when I thought of the possibilities. Now, I could envision a future. I would fall in love with this and him. Surely, abundant love and his security were enough to maintain and sustain a marriage.

When he proposed, my mom did not object. She was thrilled at the security and education he possessed. Her dream of me marrying this man was perfect. The ring was gorgeous—big and beautiful—a symbol of what would surely be a rich marriage. I felt proud and proven worthy.

I just wanted to know my future. I wanted to be cared for, and more than anything, I wanted to be loved. I had been the giver for most of my life. Now it was my turn; I would receive. In this relationship, I would have my mom's acceptance, and I'd have a man who loved and cared for me. I would be marrying well.

Unlike Cinderella, who asked her fairy godmother for help, I didn't ask anyone. I did not have the benefit of a strong, wise support system. It had always been family. After all, if my mom knew he checked all the boxes, then it was sure to be right. All my college friends, at this time, were getting married. I would be graduating college in December. It must have been the right time. He must be the right man.

Even up to the wedding, several other men had expressed great interest. I wrote them "Dear John" letters and wrestled with this. The wrestling was not necessarily these men in particular, but the fact that I was in a place of curiosity. Yet I kept thinking that perhaps it was normal and that a wedding, a marriage, would settle all this. When curiosity is present and peace is not, pay attention. It is critically important.

The wedding took place on December 21. It was a beautiful winter day in sunny California, and it was the first wedding for both families.

The dress was made to order and hand-beaded, the tiara was purchased in Europe, and a designer was in charge of the color coordination. Black tuxedo for him and the same for the groomsmen. We had a church wedding followed by a lakeside restaurant with a dinner reception, complete with a swan ice carving and multi-tiered wedding cake. And yet, it is interesting now to think back on it. The guests, except for family, were primarily friends of my parents and family. I can remember very few from his side of the family. Social connections were few and far removed. I paid little attention and truly thought, "I'm marrying him, not his family." How wrong this would later turn out.

The honeymoon was set for two weeks in Tahiti. It was planned to be a trip of a lifetime. Instead, it poured rain for the two weeks, setting the stage for the coming 26-year marriage. I now see this as foreshadowing.

Rain—we often think that every story needs a setting and that weather is part of the setting. I believe that is true. In *How to Read Literature Like a Professor,* Thomas C. Foster writes, "There is much more to it. Here is what [he] thinks: weather is never just weather. **It's never just rain.**"[10] I would agree with him. It is wise to note the weather and, in my case, especially on the honeymoon.

Returning back from the trip, we settled into his place. It was a small two-bedroom rental home owned by his mom. This brought with it some stickiness. The details are unimportant, but suffice it to say that it was her house, not ours.

Within six months, after I graduated college and we married, I found full-time work as a real estate appraiser, and he was establishing his own financial planning business. We worked hard and spent many weekends stuffing envelopes

---

[10] Foster, Thomas C. 2017. *How to Read Literature Like A Professor.* New York, NY: HarperCollins.

and mailing out cards to his potential clients. It was a difficult first year as he was under a great deal of pressure to make it through adversity as he built a business.

In the Book of Genesis, Chapter 2, it reads, "Therefore shall a man leave his father and his mother, and shall cleave unto his wife: and they shall be one flesh."[11] This was not the case for me. My husband, at the time, was still cleaving to his mother. It wasn't all his fault. It just evolved into this because her husband died years ago, and my husband was acting as an emotional caretaker to his mother. He would go to her house after work, manage her financial portfolio, and take care of his younger, often troubled adult brothers. It was expected.

In the meantime, I began to feel lonely and very sad. I was confused because I was trying so hard to develop our marriage but could not understand this arrangement. It felt like once the wedding took place and we were husband and wife, he went right back into the familiar role of "husband" to his mom. I wanted my husband to be home at the end of the day so that we could make our lives together. I wanted to cook for him and be with him. I wanted him to prioritize me first. One day, I even went back over to my parent's home and broke down, sharing with them the sadness and confusion I felt. I wanted help. My parents sent me back to my husband.

---

[11] Genesis 2:24 NKJV

We did seek professional counseling. It helped, but it did not take away his fundamental need to stay connected to his family's ingrained philosophy of work and production. His embedded message growing up was if you work and earn great money and invest it wisely, you are valuable. He would work incredibly long hours (6:00 a.m. to 7:00 p.m., maybe 6:30 p.m. if I pleaded with him) and weekends. He always worked on Saturday, which, according to him, was his most productive time. I would ask with great anticipation what time he'd be home on Saturdays as I hoped for some time with him, maybe a date night to look forward to. This left me with a lot of alone time. As a young wife who was raised to become a wife and be supportive of her husband, I was lost and became unclear of what my role as a "Mrs." was supposed to be. My dad came home every night by 5:00 and always joined us for dinner. I could not understand how this was to be my new "normal." My husband was, as I understood it, to complete me. I now know this is *not* true. A man should never complete a woman. Nor should a woman complete a man. They cannot. It is not the blueprint God designed. But, once again, I thought I'd found my Higher Power.

This, however, was not my experience. He was a man who mistakenly believed that money and producing income was the source of security—it was his answer, his HP. Marriage was not, children were not, and relationships were not.

Within five months, I began to spend extra hours at work, too. I received a lot of attention from one man in particular. Not good. It was a slippery slope headed towards tragedy and tears. Heartbreak was coming. I began to go out with associates after hours. I began to pick up alcohol and just pour my pain into more destructive avenues. I even tried cocaine a couple of times and smoking. I was becoming someone I didn't know or want to become. One night, I didn't even come home, and I remember thinking, "I don't care."

We went to a couples therapist, but I lied to her about what was really going on. I did not want to tell the truth—I wanted to just get out of the painful, lonely marriage. It hurt too much to stay and I had no idea how to fix it. Lying bought me time and removed my responsibility. I didn't really want to fix the marriage at the time. I wanted to live and let myself live on my terms, no one else's. I was hurt, angry, and rebelling against all I had been expected to be up to that point in my life. Nothing I was taught to believe made sense or seemed to provide a solid solution. All of my former Higher Powers were removed from their former altars.

In April of that same year, I moved out. I did whatever I wanted, whenever I wanted. I stayed very busy and active in my search for something else. And I became very lonely. I thought this new freedom and geographic move would be my solution. It wasn't. Every facet of my life began to unravel. I was making mistakes in my work, and my physical well-being suffered—my skin began to break out on my back, something that had never occurred before. I shopped to avoid loneliness, partied to avoid responsibility, and disconnected from everyone and everything that I valued. All of it was failing. I had lost control.

My belief that he, my husband, would be my Higher Power, that my life would be complete in marriage, was shattered. Cinderella was stripped from her gorgeous gown; while one slipper was missing (no mistake in this symbol), the other slipper was cracked, unable to be put together. It was not his fault; it was who he was and likely will always be.

One Sunday, I decided to try going back to God, to attend a church I had never been to in an unfamiliar city. It was a small but well-established Baptist church. I found my way into a pew and just tried to be present. I had no idea what I was looking for but the void I was trying to fill was huge.

What I am about to write is not likely to be believed; nevertheless, it is absolutely true. I encountered an angel. An older woman who was standing next to me in the pew, a few feet away, gently placed her hand on me and said, "Everything is going to be okay." I nodded politely but was confused. How did she know? I had never seen her before, in a church I had never entered before, and I gave no indication to her that anything was wrong. I processed this quickly and then went to turn to say something to her, but she was gone.

I believe that she was an angel because I have no other explanation. And it was that day that I got into my car and drove straight to my parents' home. I wept as I drove. I knew my dad would be home, and my mom was out of town. Since my dad had left my mom for a short time in their marriage for another woman when I was a senior in high school, I knew he would listen without judgment. He did. He could be counted on for that; he is a safe haven for me. Listening without judgment is like a stream in a desert.

Ultimately, he advised me to go back and be honest as I sought forgiveness. My parents wanted to support me as the marriage had the possibility of repair. Because I am an optimist and I easily forgive, I know that this depends on both the husband and the wife. Each has a part in making a strong marriage work. Each needs to remove ego and replace it with humility. Each needs to be honest and willing. These are all choices. But they are individual choices.

My next step, a scary and vulnerable one, was to go to my husband, confess, and ask his forgiveness, knowing very well that he did not have to accept my apology or me as his wife as I had been unfaithful.

He did. It was brutal, but he accepted me back. And I truly wanted to be married and have the life with him that we professed on our wedding day. I was committed to him. I was committed to marriage. I was committed to God.

We made some needed changes. We moved out of his mother's rental home to gain a sense of needed separation from her. We bought our first home. I changed real estate appraisal companies. We went back to a therapist for a while. I was required to have high accountability, and I did everything I was asked to do to try to regain his trust. Unfortunately, while I believed that this was taking place, that my actions, humility, and love would be enough to help repair the damage, it later showed up even years later as an unwillingness on his part to forgive. He harbored resentment. He still does.

> "As smoking is to the lungs, so is resentment to the soul; even one puff is bad for you."
> –Elizabeth Gilbert

Because I so wanted to be loved by him, accepted by him, and forgiven by him, he was still my Higher Power. I placed my life's worth in being a wife to him.

Life carried on, and we soon started a family. The American Dream was in process, or so I thought and desperately hoped.

CHAPTER 5

Parenting

Having a family can be an incredible gift, and being a mom is the most challenging career I ever attempted. It also becomes a position of worth for many women. Parenting became my next Higher Power. It was a logical transfer because my children were my focus; my husband remained who he was, and work remained his Higher Power.

I remember my first pregnancy well. Leading up to the positive pregnancy test, my husband was reluctant. He had this idea, this false security, about having $10,000 dollars in the bank. It was a vicious cycle that he circled again and again. In fact, this was his continual "thorn in the flesh." A thorn I could never help him pull out, and I sure tried. His Higher Power was earning and managing money. It was his reason for waking up. This meant us postponing starting a family for a while until he finally relented. I was so ready to be a mother and knew that having $10,000 dollars in the bank was not the solution to life's challenges. But one day, I was given literally life-giving news that we were expecting our first child. I was beyond thrilled! It felt miraculous to me. I still believe it is a miracle to be a mother. I was always cognizant of that truth.

In May of 1989, I gave birth to our first daughter, Mia. It was a time of great joy. She was the first grandchild and niece, and she was welcomed with an abundance of love and care. She lacked for nothing.

In December of that same year, we flew to Hawaii for Christmas with my family. My parents own a lovely condominium, yet it was one of the most difficult trips ever, not because of our baby but because of my husband. He was angry and filled with stress over money again. He was lashing out at me in front of my family because he was anxious over the lack of money he thought he needed to be okay. Being on vacation and not at work escalated his anxiety.

I remember parking the stroller in front of a large waterfall and feeling fed up and angry with his perspective on our lives versus his stress over money. I could not understand how he could be so hung up on it rather than just being present with us in paradise with free accommodations and content with having enough rather than a certain number of zeros in the bank to feel okay. This became a constant source of contention for us.

I understood that his self-worth was tied to his ability to make money. He had a conditional relationship with his own mom that bred this behavior and a false sense of who he was. I thought I could change this. I was very wrong. But, nonetheless, I tried with every fiber of my being.

I would go to many measures to keep the peace and seek his approval, especially once we both decided that I would stay home as a homemaker after our second child was about six months old. We both believed this to be the best decision for our family, yet a financially challenging one. I was a woman who knew hard work well and was willing to do whatever it took to follow this path for our family. I also understood that he was doing what he thought was best for our family. I still believe it was the best decision for our children, and I loved being a homemaker and full-time mom.

Considering I still had outstanding student loans, I decided I would not let this be my husband's burden to carry. I became resourceful and offered our home and my mothering skills to care for other children, primarily children of close friends whom I met in my daughter's Mommy and Me Pre-school. It was a success and supplemented our family income. Additionally, I set a goal to pay off my student loans within a few years as a result of my income.

While the above was a logical and practical approach to a debt I owed, the debt I was never able to pay was my husband's quest to earn more. The constant need to sacrifice. Owning a home that needed lots of work did not help.

Our home was a true fixer-upper. We knew this when we purchased it, but, like so many couples, it became a vacuum for money. Everything needed replacement, it seemed. I made some unreasonable, foolish decisions when it came to this house. I hired a very expensive decorator. I insisted on her as she was my mom's decorator, and I was disillusioned by the idea that we could afford her. We did afford her but it came at a price we struggled to pay. This, I know, caused my husband undue stress. I regret that now. Again, now I see that it was connected to my turning over my need to have the house beautiful so that others would think well of me. I tied our home to acceptance.

Somehow, back then, I believed that my home was linked together with my personal worth. Things, like a house, became other sources of a Higher Power. It mattered to me what people thought about our house rather than about a relationship or how our home could just be a source of sweet hospitality. I thought it needed to be a place of perfection. Perfection later showed up as one of my primary character defects.

Saving more money to please my husband came to be an absolute requirement. After four children, I became a student of coupon cutting, making costumes, shopping at discounted stores, and waiting in lines at medical care facilities that offered free health care for children. Since my husband was self-employed as a Certified Financial Planner (CFP) and an enrolled tax agent (later on), we did not have the luxury of medical benefits, only major medical coverage. I worked hard at home, and he worked hard at his office. I went to great lengths to save money where I could, as this became part of my job requirement.

Vacationing evolved from tent camping to buying an old travel trailer, allowing us to create lasting memories with the kids. I started searching for one and then worked very hard to convince my husband to look at it. He was very skeptical but eventually relented. Thankfully, we had it long enough for him to experience its benefits, and later, we decided to replace it with a new one. We cherished many memories in those RVs. When the kids outgrew the bunks in the second trailer, and we began to save for bigger trips that required airfare, we prepared to sell it. Talia, my daughter, looked at me with confusion and remarked, "Mommy, you can't sell the trailer; that's like selling all our memories." It broke my heart, but I also understood the priceless memories that it imprinted on her heart. It was one of the best investments we ever made.

As the kids were about to start school, I sought out what I thought would be the best educational path for them. I researched. I read. I explored several schools. My first choice was a private school, and after visiting it and calling my husband from the parking lot, excited and convinced that it was the best environment for our daughter, he informed me that, while it might be the best choice for her, we couldn't afford it. This became a recurring theme that I would hear frequently and throughout the rest of the marriage. I should have paid more attention to this from the outset. In the words of Maya Angelou, "When people show you who they are, believe them."

Reflecting on the early stages of our marriage, it began with our need to buy a simple coffee table in our first home. I found a crazy octagon-shaped table at a garage sale for $10.00. "Oh well," I thought, "at least we have one." It progressed to keeping our avocado green, matted carpet in our first home despite having a buyer's carpet allowance. Things promised to be replaced and deemed "temporary" became permanent until I found a way to replace them. It became my responsibility to create ways to make life's purchases a reality. He hated to spend money. It was like he valued deprivation. My dad used to tease him by saying he would stay at work so that he could get the last dollar off the street. It was sad and actually not a laughing matter because it was true.

It was an exhausting role, but I gained something I needed. I gained purpose and personal satisfaction in finding what I believed best for our children. And he likely believed he was doing his best by providing for our children, working six to seven days a week.

Not all was horrible. I honed my cooking and hostess skills. This filled my tank of approval, which translated into love. I had dear friends who were at home raising their children, and we had many park days and beach days. I loved being home with my children. My husband provided this opportunity for me and for our children. But, I was slowly losing my sense of self. I just kept shifting the target of approval to align with the moving arrow.

Since the cost of private school was beyond our means, I committed to homeschooling our children for several years. Later, I transitioned them into a private school where they were homeschooled two days a week and attended school for three days. Once again, this was a financial strain, according to my husband, so I applied as a teacher, got hired, and our children could attend the school at a fraction of the cost. The same scenario occurred when our oldest daughter was about to begin high school. She wished to join her friends at the private school, but my husband said it was impossible. I made an appointment with the principal and explained our situation and my teaching experience. He offered me a teaching position! As a result, we were able to enroll all four of our children in the school, and I worked as an English teacher.

For many years, I drove an old 1989 Suburban truck that had a bumper sticker that read "Home School Bus." My friends and I laughed about it. They used to tease me and say he would bury me in it. Functionality was paramount. Frugality was a necessity. Forging a way was the key to that lockbox.

My tenacity was ever-present. It had to be if I was to survive in the marriage and provide what I believed was best for my children's well-being. I was a force behind and in front of them, not because I wanted my way necessarily, but because I was resourceful and knew it was up to me to create what I believed to be great opportunities for them. It was not without mistakes.

Parenting became the arena where I confronted my greatest character defects and did not often manage them well. As my responsibilities increased with each of my children, these defects of character became highlighted. As a married woman whose husband lived as a workaholic, I often felt like a single mother, doing the best I knew at the time. However, this time was littered with many regrettable and poor decisions, not because I was a poor parent, but because I was pushing myself beyond my limits, trying to accomplish more than was realistically possible, and striving to do it all exceptionally well. I took the children to church, homeschooled them, engaged them in sports and club activities, and devoted myself entirely to being a full-time mother. But the inability to meet all these needs was beyond me. This eventually paved the road for me to become a flaming codependent and, later, an alcoholic. It was a continuous quest for validation and love, a relentless pursuit that became a constant nemesis.

Even today, parenting is still tricky and puzzling, especially with my adult children. I frequently turn to *The Language of Letting Go* by Melody Beattie.[12] I need her wise words to keep me honest as I often try so hard to make "it" happen. I need to do my part, as Melody says, "in relaxed, peaceful harmony." Then I need to let it go because when I learn to let "it" happen, it ends up how "it" will happen anyway. I exhaust myself and wear my heart and mind out trying to achieve certain desired results with my kids. I see that we each have a part in the relationship, and while they no longer need me, I love them and hope that they will want a healthy, safe, kind, and supportive relationship with me. I do. However, I cannot emotionally stretch myself beyond healthy limits to force that to happen. There is nothing healthy about that. It is a choice made by each of us out of love and not need. Writing this weighs heavily on my heart. Why? Because regrettably, my four grown adult children have chosen not to maintain a relationship with me. The dynamics of this are truly dark, rooted in resentment, selfishness, pain, and pride. These emotions do not stem from me but from my ex-husband and, sadly, my three sisters.

---

[12] Beattie, Melody. *The Language of Letting Go*. Hazelden, 1990.

The silver lining is that I continue to see that they, like me, need a Higher Power, and I am not it. Every day, I pray that they all become willing to see that and that their adult lives are transformed from darkness to light. I hope for a day when they will know the truth, understanding that the truth will set them free. And, in the meantime, I pray for my heart to be a soft landing for all of them supported by grace.

CHAPTER 6

The Codependent

Codependent is a foreign term for many. It was for me. What does it mean? While Google has lots of smart ways to define it, I will use one I researched and then further explain based on my own experience with codependency. According to an article titled "What is Codependency" by Wendy Rose Gould and reviewed by David Susman, PhD, codependency can come in all shapes and sizes and varying levels of severity. "Foundationally, it is due to a poor concept of self and poor boundaries, including an inability to have an opinion or say no," says Dr. Mark Mayfield, a licensed professional counselor (LPC). He adds that codependency can develop in all sorts of relationships, such as parent-child, partner-partner, spouse-spouse, and even coworker-boss.[13]

As a child, a parent's typical response when their children question their authority or judgment is often "no." As

---

[13] https://www.verywellmind.com/what-is-codependency-5072124

a teenager whose natural maturation includes questioning and seeking answers, a simple "yes" or "no" is not so simple. Reasoning is often helpful and sometimes needed. Making space for forward-thinking and decision-making is how teens learn. In my family situation, I was not allowed to say "no" in most situations involving my mom. I was really not allowed to express my opinion, question things, or use my voice for fear that it would be interpreted as a challenge. This, as I see it now, cultivated codependent issues in me. They were easily primed for development and were like yeast in a ball of rising dough.

What difference does it make? To struggle with codependency? I mean, isn't it good to care about others and put them first? It starts off innocently. It is "cunning, baffling, powerful."[14] It felt good to have people tell me that I was a giver, a great confidant, readily available. Until it didn't. Until I was the last one on the list of care to be cared about.

This pattern trickled into seemingly every area of my life. Friendships were sometimes compromised; my dating relationships with men lasted longer than they should have, my work relationships did not know how to simply separate business and pleasure, and my children needed me to be a parent, not a friend, as they developed into teenagers. Boundaries, for me, were messy. I wanted to be liked and

---

[14] W., Bill. *Alcoholics Anonymous*. Fourth ed., Alcoholics Anonymous World Services, 2001.

approved by seemingly everyone. People were my Higher Power in a multitude of ways. When children are young, their needs are fairly simple. When they begin to mature and work themselves into adolescence, their needs are far more complex. They seem to need more fences and rules and less explaining.

My husband, at the time, was comfortable with our children when they were young and played well with them. He was good at it. I appreciated how he made it look so easy when I was physically exhausted from meeting their constant needs. Playing with them in the pool, taking them out to play golf, watching movies on the couch with them, washing the cars together—these were things he did that well when he was home.

When they began to enter the teenage years, it was very different. He could not connect with them well. He lacked the emotional ability to empathize with their experiences. He did not know how to just ask them how they were doing and really listen so they felt understood. He also did not physically seem to show love. He was more concerned with outcomes and results than just seeing them for who they were as individuals through acceptance, love, and care. I, of course, had my shortcomings as a mom. I was often more preoccupied with keeping of the house and order than playing with my children. I regret that now. It is so clear. The time went by so fast, and man, oh man, I wish I had invested a lot more time just being with the kids and laughing with them. I was frequently too concerned with trivial things (housekeeping, order, controlling the universe!). This was another form of a Higher Power: things versus people.

I know that it was connected to my codependency. I wanted so badly to be Superwoman. I falsely believed that if I was her, I'd get the acknowledgment and, therefore, love, I was striving to reach.

My then-husband's role of being emotionally unavailable to our children, especially our oldest daughter, was detrimental to her well-being. She became promiscuous and rebellious against all we had taught and fortified. And it manifested itself in sad ways in our other children as they matured from children to teens. One became a gaming addict, another sought unhealthy ways to calm her ADHD, and one became a worried high achiever. While this is a mountain we all climb through various avenues, we each select the tools we need to survive. It comes with no judgment on my part today. I understand that life is certainly not without bumps and wrinkles. Some get ironed out, and some are just stubborn, like stains you'd like to remove.

This was so scary when it was taking place. I felt hopeless and helpless. Yes, we tried family counseling and church. Yes, we had boundaries and consequences. Yes, we prayed and tried to seek answers. But it was too late, and the damage was already done. Both parents, in this case, need to do the work and take the steps necessary to bring about change. You cannot quickly fix a damaged relationship. When you crack a crystal vase, it can be glued, but the cracks are still present.

I write this part of my story so as to inform you, the reader, and maybe save you and your child the tragedy I lived and did not know how to fix. I really tried every resource to make a change, but I came to learn late that I could only change myself. And that I mattered, not just my husband. I protected him at the expense of my life and my honesty with my children. They never knew the depths of the hurt or the balancing I tried to save the marriage. This was a mistake. I should have communicated much earlier with the help of a professional marriage and family therapist about what was taking place. I thought that protecting my kids from the truth was best. I thought that I should protect their image of their dad. I was wrong. I paid dearly for this later. I'm still paying. And I believe they, my children who are now adults, are still hurting. Knowing the truth sets us free, but it often comes with pain.

The sun rose and set on our first daughter, being the firstborn child. I wanted her to be without fault. Impossible, I know. When she fell short, I would correct her. I tried to help her take ownership of her choices, but there were many times when I believed her to be telling the truth when she was not. She had a streak of rancorous intent in her. It seemed like she was born with it. I now believe this is a facet of alcoholism, but I knew nothing about it then. She always wanted more of everything. It was like a thirst that could not be quenched. And when she didn't get it, bitterness and bad came out.

On day two after her baby brother's birth, she bit him hard. On another occasion, she told her brother and sisters that they were adopted. They were not. Still more, she lied about a horse she wanted to ride and lease from the owner so that her best friend, who had already placed an interest, would not have first rights to it. I painfully discovered much of this and more after the facts. In the process of it, I defended her. I wanted to believe her and protect her. I did not know that my decisions to do this would be one of the worst mom decisions I would make and need to own.

As she entered her teenage years, she began to become, as mentioned earlier, promiscuous. I won't engage in the details, but suffice it to say it was chronic. Here is the part I hate and humbly admit: after battling rules and contracts with her, I caved into her wishes and life choices. I actually convinced my husband to allow her to bring her then high school boyfriend on vacation with us and have their own room. This was coming from a woman who was a church-going, Bible study gal and lover of God. My decisions reflected everything I was not. As I read this, I feel such sadness and regret. It was wrong. I was wrong. I wronged her.

This led me to further worse decisions. By the time she was 18, I allowed her to be my wine-drinking buddy. Shameful of me, yes, it was. It makes me cringe as I write this. When I hear parents say that they would rather let their underage kids drink at home than go out and party, I want to say, "Please don't." It is a huge mistake; they need boundaries as teens and will have those invitations soon enough in college and careers. Do not be a parent who gives them this invitation. Don't ever forget that you are the parent. It is a huge responsibility, and no matter how much they badger you, do not cave in to their adolescent manipulation. They will likely respect you later. They are counting on you to say, "No. I love you. No." They do not need to understand. They cannot because they are not adults. They are teens trying to figure out life, and they need their parents to make some of these decisions for them.

While she was in private high school, she had a lot of male attention. She was a beautiful young woman, and this was noticed by many young men. She was nominated for homecoming queen and never lacked interest from guys. Insanely, I tried to manage her life. I was trying to control her because I could not control my own lifeless marriage. Crazy, yes. Codependency at its peak. Insanity running wild. She became my Higher Power.

I was so empty in my loveless, performance-based marriage that I transferred my worth into her life. My value as a mom was tied to her successes and failures. It was sick and distorted. I can only say that I channeled my pain into creating the life I wished I had into hers. It was wrong, very wrong. The damage felt unrepairable. Even years later, after making my amends to her several times with complete humility, I do not have a relationship with her. It is truly a tragedy. I wish I could have a do-over, but that has not been granted. She is not willing. I pray for it and hope that one day it will be different, but today, it is a broken relationship. Only a willingness on her part to forgive, with God's help, will make that possible.

She began to get deeper and deeper into sex, drugs, and alcohol. I would find bottles of Jack Daniels in the file cabinet; she became bulimic, rebellious, and unwilling to adhere to any standards we set or any consequences we gave. Respect for us as her parents was gone. Nothing worked.

When I would frantically ask my husband to step in, he would become unglued, angry, or just complacent with her behavior. He could not control her any better than I could. Of course, I now believe this is because he was too late to enter her life as a parent. He had made too many decisions along the way of her growing up that did not show his care in her life as she needed it. His solution was typically money. Our lives had become unmanageable. This deeply affected our other three children, as all the attention was centered around our oldest daughter. I feel great remorse over this. We stole time from them as we over-focused on our oldest, out-of-control, hurting daughter.

Daily, I would sit on our family room couch. Early every morning, I'd cry and plead for God's help. I was desperate for a solution. Every day, I would promise God that today would be different, but every day, the next morning, I was unable to change. I needed help. I was powerless to change my daughter. I had made her my Higher Power.

At one point, my husband and I escaped to a bed and breakfast inn. I was cognizant of the need to have time away, and because I could make it happen, I planned these getaways several times a year. Exhausted from the rounds I had with our daughter, we checked into our room. I excused myself for a much-needed jacuzzi bath. I filled up the tub with hot water up to my neck and turned on the jets. I began to feel a deep relief that started in my gut and rose to my chest. Before I knew it, I was sobbing uncontrollably. It was unstoppable. It overtook me as I felt all the pain from inside my body rise and expel from my person. Never have I cried so hard. My body was heaving; I was convulsing. This was the start of my awareness and acceptance. Change was imperative. We returned home, and I became willing to seek God for help, not my husband.

One day, my youngest sister called. She had a suggestion. She had a friend who was going to a 12-step group for codependents. I had no idea what that was, but it didn't matter. I was falling apart at the seams; I needed surgery on the mind and heart. I would do anything.

In March of 2006, I went to my first Codependents Anonymous meeting. I had no expectations but felt relief in being in a room with other women who struggled with the same dysfunction. While I listened to the Serenity Prayer and the readings of the steps from the Big Book of AA, I began to feel some relief. They said, "Keep coming back. It works if you work it, and it won't if you don't." They were right.

While I wanted an answer and then to move on, this would not be the case. I was so codependent that I tried going every other week so that my husband would not be angry and I would be home to cook dinner. At this point, any one of our older kids could have managed dinner. But, I was emotionally ill and needed a meeting every week.

I learned the steps of recovery from codependency, and I found a sponsor who led me along the way and met with me to share her experience, strength, and hope. I learned boundaries and how to care about myself and not to be a caretaker for others, especially my daughter. I learned that I was enabling my husband's behavior as a workaholic. I learned that my needs mattered and I was not supposed to take care of everyone else. I mattered to God.

Things were about to change because I was learning to take ownership of my life and not manage everyone else's.

When our eldest daughter was eighteen, in July of that year, we asked her to move out. She had an opportunity to move to Arizona with her boyfriend at the time, and he was moving to begin college. She left. It was the best decision for all of us.

Unfortunately, my husband, unbeknownst to me, sent her supplemental money without me knowing. This was after we had decided what was needed and what was wise to do for her financially. Later, I found out that she was selling her medication for her ADHD, and still, my husband continued financially supplementing her poor decisions. At one point, one of my younger, more honest daughters became exasperated. She knew more than I did and, angrily and righteously, asked why we were contributing to our daughter's addictive habits. I was infuriated with my husband as we had already established together what we believed was wise. He went behind me to send her money. This put him in the position of hero and me in the position of bitch. From this point on, I let him manage her as it was clear that my boundaries for her were not respected nor supported.

Shortly after our divorce, she made a clear boundary to not contact me. I know this was the direct result of my learning and keeping boundaries with her. While I made sincere efforts year after year on Christmas and on her birthday, her last text to me was, "Stop fucking texting me."

Fast forward to May of 2017, when she graduated college. I received an announcement in the mail. While I was not invited to the ceremony, her dad was. I sent a card and a gift. My two younger daughters said that I need not, but I wanted to because I love her. I always will. I am truly happy for her to have accomplished this for herself and her future. I am sad she has decided to remove me, her mom, from her life, but that is no longer for me to resist or think sadly through. My life does not lack purpose. She was removed, thanks to my recovery, from the HP position. She will always be my daughter. I will always be her mom. Nothing can change that, and I pray one day, she returns to God first and then to me.

I sent her cards and gifts at Christmas but without acknowledgement from her for eight years. I have since decided, with the counsel of others, that she cannot deny my efforts were consistent and caring. I cannot bridge the gap for her. I now live my life as a living amends and trust that she is exactly where she needs to be for today. I pray for God's protection over her and that recovery becomes a part of her life. I believe she is worth it, and I love her. I always will. Nothing she can do will ever change my heart of love for her.

Codependency is a horrible way to live life. It places our worth in the hands of others. It manifests itself in the destruction of ourselves **and** of those we love. It is not loving to care for others. It is loving to care about them. We, however, are to care for ourselves first, or we have little to give to those we love. I learned this the hard way.

CHAPTER 7

Men

"Be the woman God sees you to be. It's a lot."
–Doug Fields

Men. The Higher Power, if not THE (seemingly) Highest Power for a woman.

Recently, I received a voicemail from a gal whom I met in Codependents Anonymous. Much time had passed since we had seen one another. We were connected, though, via social media as the years slipped away. She was a regular attender. She is a medical doctor, yet, as I have learned, addiction has no barriers; it does not discriminate, and she needed help.

When I called her back, I heard a very familiar story of a woman in absolute dire pain over a man. She shared how they had a very special connection; they really had fun together, sailed together, and that even sex was not just sex, that they made love. It felt like a true connection. But they had been through several break-ups, and perhaps this time it was over, but she was hanging on for hope and needed me to listen and understand. I did. I really did.

As she shared for about thirty minutes, she weaved in that alcohol was a problem. It reared its ugly head over and over and was a source of her recklessness and emotional outbursts in the relationship, even physical outbursts. All, in my opinion, was rooted in fear. Fear of losing the man. I listened carefully to her story. I well understood her fear.

I asked her if she wanted my feedback. She said yes.

Okay, I thought. Here is where sharing my experience, strength, and hope needs to show up in a most understanding and truthful way. The truth is … I knew the root problem. Fear. Fear of not being loved. It is terrifying. It is because it's what we most need—to be loved and known. And when we believe we have it, and it comes in the shape of a man for a woman or a woman for a man, we want it to be forever. We want our life to be anchored in it. We think it is THE thing that will fill our void.

When that "anchor" is moved or removed, we find everything else in our lives nearly meaningless. The results are baffling. We turn to all kinds of coping mechanisms: alcohol, drugs, food, sugar, and shopping, and the list goes on. Just pick your drug of choice, and you get to numb or perhaps put a temporary hold on what will need to be managed. The horrible part is that it feels and often becomes unmanageable.

We will call friends and try to create a mental file for every minuscule of hope. We will do just about anything to will the relationship back and then circle around why we can live without them, but it always seems to come back to a desperate plea within ourselves and maybe to God to give it back, to have that guy back. This was the case with this particular woman and thousands like her.

I also read that the term "Escalation of Commitment" happens to many of us. It means that we have a tendency to continue to invest in someone even if it's years and we have no progress and even if it is getting worse. We tend to focus on how much time has been invested in a relationship as if it were proportional to how much hope we should have for its success, and we overlook the actual quality of the relationship itself.

We do not often know how to define love. It is frequently out of need that we stay because we are in fear of losing the guy, of being alone, or of the pain that can come from being single.

Afterwards, I invited her to a Twelve Step meeting where we reunited in person. She looked so fragile and physically hurt. The left side of her face was scabbed from what looked like a rough date with asphalt. I did not ask what happened. I hugged her and welcomed her. I introduced her to my sponsor, Sue. It was a great meeting. The next day, she texted me. "So good to see you. Enjoyed the meeting. Right now, I'm feeling a peace beyond understanding."

Three days later, a new text. More sad news about the death of her sister on the other side of the U.S. and that they had not spoken in ten years. She went on to say that she was supposed to go out to dinner with a guy who is supposedly a friend but always tries to pressure her to have sex with him, and she doesn't want to. She felt "all alone."

It's, sadly, not a new story for me to hear from a woman. I hear different versions, often.

I wrote back how sorry I was to hear all of it. I made suggestions like canceling the dinner plans with a man who sounds like a loser and a selfish jerk. That there is no wisdom in adding more pain to her life.

I understood that she felt alone, but that is simply not true. Feelings are like clouds—they pass. Perhaps, in the absence of a man who is not willing or unable to be in a relationship with her today (her ex), she is able, if willing, to call out to her Higher Power. He is with her. That is the truth. It is written: He is the Alpha and Omega.

My final suggestion was that she go, herself, to a Twelve Step meeting. By the way, all this took place on Christmas Day. I also asked her to call me the following day if she wanted to go to a meeting with me. She did.

I encouraged her progress and called her. We planned to meet at another meeting the next day. She was all set to go but then texted me during the meeting that she missed it. She asked for another meeting opportunity, and I sent her the Meeting Guide app. I did not hear from her until two months later.

She showed up at one of my women's meetings. She now had to come. She needed a court card signed. She had a DUI. This was the result of trying to fill her void with a man as her HP and then alcohol to subdue the pain. She, like many men and women, became a subject of "King Alcohol," as the Big Book of Alcoholics Anonymous states.

A spiritual solution is essential if we want change. Spirituality is a part of getting in touch with reality. But, if she or any other woman I work with is to find God, the desire must come from within. It only requires a willingness to believe in a Power greater than oneself and that one lives by spiritual principles. For me, that is the Bible. It just cannot be another man.

The problem, for many like her, is that it becomes "baffling, cunning, powerful."[15] We cannot picture life without alcohol, just like we cannot picture life without a man.

And it usually goes from bad to worse … The last time I saw her was in a meeting. She had to be there after receiving

---

[15] W., Bill. Alcoholics Anonymous. Fourth ed., Alcoholics Anonymous World Services, 2001.

a DUI while stalking the man, and now he has a restraining order against her, and it has become progressively worse. Her car ignited on fire while she drove it on a flat and then on the rim. She broke her arm. She is likely to lose her medical license. She continues to blame the man. She continues to go in and out of the rooms of recovery. I hope that she comes back and stays to do the work. If she does, she will likely stay. If she doesn't, who knows the destruction that awaits?

Like this woman, I have been on a long, circuitous journey to get the man who would be my solution to security and love.

- -

I wonder how your search began. The search to find a life solution through a relationship.

My own search for Mr. Wonderful started when my mom began reading me the fairy tales of princes and princesses. I wanted to have one and to be one! It was indeed a fairy tale, but it seemed so possible. Books, movies, commercials, magazines, videos, and social media are filled with these ideals. Who doesn't want to be swept off her feet by a handsome prince on a white horse? These male images come in all different versions, along with the "horse" or car they drive, but the world shapes us to seek them. And we will often go to maximal measures to get them. I did.

And it's not their fault. The men. They are portrayed as superhuman beings. They need to be courageous yet kind, protectors yet comforting, providers yet givers, sexy yet faithful, handsome yet humble. This is just a list of many sought after attributes we, women, often search for and then decide it's not exactly what we envisioned. Maybe we are the problem. Maybe we need to seek a different source of fulfillment. Maybe men are meant to complement us rather than complete us.

When a man becomes your HP, your security and purpose lie with them. Big mistake. It can also appear true, and that was my experience. I placed my value, who I was, on my role as a wife. I really believed he was my pot of gold at the end of the rainbow. Why? If you are reading this with any curiosity, especially if you are young, in your 20s or early 30s, then I want to be clear. Never let a man you commit to in a significant relationship diminish in any way who you are, your personal goals, or your ambitions. Never. That person should compliment you and encourage you to be the best version of yourself. They should rejoice in your gifts and your growth professionally and personally. If they don't, something is wrong with them, not you.

I wish I knew when I was younger to take serious consideration as to the why's of a relationship. Maybe that sounds dumb or simple, but it was way bigger than I had understood in my 20s. Consider carefully completing an honest inventory of a relationship. It is not complicated; it is relatively simple. I just did not know that then. My suggestion is to write a list of what your ideal mate would be like. Next, write a list of what you are bringing into the relationship, assets, and liabilities. Last, what are your deal-breakers or non-negotiable issues in a relationship? After this is completed, call a trusted and wise, unbiased person (I met with a more mature male and, later, separately, with my female therapist) to review the inventory and discuss it thoroughly together. I also numbered the ideals from most important to least. I asked myself, how does the person I am in a relationship with and considering marrying match up to these ideals? I also learned by meeting with this wise male friend that some of my non-negotiables were actually not nonnegotiable when asked a bit more about them. For example, I thought that drinking alcohol would be non-negotiable, but after further consideration, I realized that if it was on a special occasion and he was not an alcoholic, it would be okay. This friend helped me weed through my list.

If nothing changes in the relationship after this inventory is spelled out, will you be enough? Don't sell yourself and your purpose for someone else, especially out of fear that you will be alone. It's not true. We deserve whatever we are willing to accept. DO NOT be driven by fear. Trust and rely on your HP. For me, that is God. He is the solution. You are specifically made. You need to believe that God wants this or something better. Get honest with yourself. Get honest with God. Get clarity. "For God has not given us a spirit of fear, but of power and love and discipline."[16]

He may be perfect the way he is for him. You are perfect the way you are for you. (I recognize that "perfect" here means that you, like me, are a work in progress, not necessarily "perfect.") This does not mean you are best together. Love is not always the answer to fix it all, but it works both ways. We need to love who we are first. Then, someone else. It is a natural manifestation of the love we have for ourselves. We can love someone but not need to change or maybe accept the behaviors of another—it needs to work both ways. If not, it becomes exhausting and frustrating. It will affect the quality of life you want and need. It may even affect your life's purpose.

Be okay with not being in a relationship for some time if that is what it is for now or for a while. Make the most of it by connecting yourself in new ways to your HP and those He brings into your life to add joy and growth to who you are and who you are becoming. Friends can be incredible sources of kindness, fun, support, unselfishness, and love. Find them. Be one. You will be a better person because of them. My girlfriends are the rubies of my life.

Secondly, live purposefully in your career or given area of service. It, for me, became my reason to wake up every

---

[16] 2 Timothy 1:7 NKJV

morning. It was not for him, the man. It was for what God had, I believe, intrinsically placed in me and what gave meaning to my life. When I stay in service, I don't have time to think too much about myself or the thoughts that surf my brain.

"Remember that the first quality of greatness is service. In a way, God is the greatest servant of all because He is always waiting for us to call on Him to help us in all good endeavors." Living a life of service, my husband tells me, is the finest life we can live. "We are here on earth to serve others. It is the beginning and the end of our real worth."[17] "You should strive for a union between your purposes in life and the purposes of the Divine Principle directing the universe. There is no bond of union on earth to compare with the union between a human soul and God. Priceless beyond all earth's rewards is that union. In merging your heart and mind of the Higher Power, a oneness of purpose results, which only those who experience it can even dimly realize. That oneness of purpose puts you in harmony with God and with all others who are trying to do His will."[18]

I learned that my security rests in God alone—not in other people, not in my circumstances. But I did not know this until later. The world I grew up in and was surrounded by showed me that he, the man or a husband, was my rock

---

[17] *Twenty-Four Hours a Day*. Hazelden Publishing, 2020.
[18] *Twenty-Four Hours a Day*. Hazelden Publishing, 2020.

and my world. And he was very good at creating that precept for me to believe. So were my parents. So was my church. So were those we knew as married couples. No one knew the sadness I felt. The internal pain I suffered. It was like a dark light was consuming my spirit of love and life.

Depending on God, at the time, felt like walking on a tightrope and not knowing there was a safety net underneath. God was not, at this time, my Stable Partner. I thought it was a husband. I thought it was supposed to be a man. And that I was not complete without one.

But God is a rescuer. He showed me the way to Him. He brought me toward recovery. With time and willingness, he put the stones that make the mosaic of my life into a worthwhile and a mixed-up yet beautiful pattern.

"Our next function is to grow in understanding and effectiveness."[19]

Today, I am an ex-wife. A very grateful ex-wife. I am grateful that I am no longer married to my first husband. He, likely, is grateful not to be married to me. We are not a match. We were not for a long time, but acceptance of that, for me, took a very l-o-n-g time. Our marriage was an ongoing problem that I kept trying to change. It was like a tutor who is always by your side. The learning possibilities are limited only by your willingness to be teachable. I needed

---

[19] W., Bill. *Alcoholics Anonymous*. Fourth ed., Alcoholics Anonymous World Services, 2001.

to get that I could not change him, and he could not change me. It took me w-a-y long to get that and accept it before change would come. I later learned God's will, not mine, be done.

"Although the Lord gives you the bread of adversity and the water of affliction, your teachers will be hidden no more; with your own eyes, you will see them. Whether you turn to the right or to the left, your ears will hear a voice behind you, saying, 'This is the way; walk in it.'"[20]

After 26 years of marriage, four children whom we both dearly love, and my decision to be in recovery in 2006 for codependency, I filed for divorce. I became the change I wanted. I became willing to see the possibility of light. Thank God. I became fully aware and accepting of my marriage for what it was, who he is, and who I am. I wanted emotional connection and time; he wanted significance through his business and financial portfolio.

If you are a parent reading this, I want to make something very clear. Resentment and bitterness have no place in our lives. DO your own work with God on this. DO NOT drag your pain or unforgiveness into your kid's lives. Love them. Let them have a relationship with your ex and honor it. You may not like it or them, but do not take your fears or anger and transfer it to your children. It is powerful. It is destructive. It is wrong. And if you are a family member or

---
[20] Isaiah 30:20–21 NKJV

friend, do not offer your opinion. You have no idea what it is truly like to be them. "You never really understand a person until you consider things from his point of view—until you climb into his skin and walk around in it."[21]

It is a major challenge for some of us to give ourselves something we've never had. I continued to be challenged to find what I wanted for years after a 26-year marriage. I would not learn my solution to this until I understood my codependency and my alcoholism. My next step was to become a credentialed teacher. More knowledge, but not the complete answer.

---

[21] Lee, Harper. To Kill A Mockingbird. Arrow Books, 2010.

CHAPTER 8

Career (Teacher)

Through an interesting chain of events, approximately three years prior to my filing for the divorce, many positive changes took place for me. Although I graduated from college as an economics and business major, I later changed careers to education. This was a direct result of homeschooling my own children. Who would have thought this would happen from that decision? God knew. It was part of a divine plan.

As I mentioned in an earlier chapter, I taught our children at home for a season. It was a precious time for me with the kids, and while I believe it went on longer than was best, it was a gift for me to have the opportunity to be their teacher and to create a path that would later become my heart's desire and valued work.

After being hired as a teacher at the private school where we enrolled all four of our children, I came to realize that I loved teaching. I did not have teaching credentials because private schools are not required to have them by the State of California. But, I began to see the personal and professional need for this.

Two years into my teaching at the private high school level, I made the decision to enroll in a teaching credential program. This took a lot of research and determination. School was a thing of the past, and I had much to figure out in order to apply and be accepted. Twenty years had passed since I attended college, but I believed it was my true course.

Being accepted to Vanguard University was a gift that I did not fully understand at the time, but it paid off lucrative dividends later. It was a scary step though. A very scary step that produced huge feelings of inferiority. I was accepted but put on academic probation as my GPA was not high enough from college (20 years prior) to convince them I was a strong candidate. I understood this.

Two years later, I graduated with a degree in secondary education. The next big step was taking the CSET examinations. Thankfully, because I was a current private school teacher and current in the curriculum, on my first attempt, I passed all the exams. It was a huge confirmation for me.

My next endeavor was to complete teacher observation at a public high school. I was intimidated when I walked into the school office without an appointment and asked if I might be able to talk with the assistant principal of curriculum. He would be the one I needed to ask if a current English teacher would be willing to allow me to observe their classes. As it worked out, I was placed in the class of a brilliant and creative teacher. Her name was Cristina. I was mesmerized by her kindness and absolute love for literature and teaching. She became a conduit of inspiration and creative teaching for me.

We became friends. One day, as we walked the Dana Point harbor, she asked me what my monthly salary was at the private school. When I told her, she gasped. She then said, "What are you, a martyr?" I had not thought of it that way. I loved what I did, and the financial reward of it didn't really matter to me. While the amount I earned was not important to me at the time, her question gave me the courage and encouragement to apply to her school. At the next opportunity, I applied.

It was a time of great hope for me and a time of trust in God to see what would happen. My teacher-friend who gave me the information to apply was also the wife of the English department chair. He, along with the assistant principal of curriculum and the district, would determine if I was hired. It was a true test of my integrity to not contact her and ask her to use her influence to get me the position. I knew I could, but I chose not to and trust the outcome.

The day I received the phone call offering me the position was one I will always remember. I could not believe it.

It felt too good to be true. To hear that I, a woman who had been a stay-at-home mom for more than ten years, a homeschool teacher who went back to school to change careers, who had been suppressed by a lack of financial freedom from her husband, was hired as a credentialed English teacher in a public school with benefits and a pension was almost unbelievable. I was thrilled beyond my biggest dreams. This opened the door to what would become my next greatest purpose. It was not, as I previously thought, connected to a man.

I have a Bachelor of Economics and Business degree. I have a master's in education. I have a teaching credential in English. This might indicate that I am smart. It might indicate that I know some stuff. It might indicate I academically surpassed others. My second-grade teacher, a nun, would never have seen this. She would have testified, "Definitely ... not." My fifth-grade teacher would have said, "Ehem ... no." My high school academic advisor had to chase me down a week before graduation to be sure I was going to have enough credits to walk with my class. Suffice it to say that it was a mysterious path to becoming a teacher, but I've been on a path of learning all my life, and while it was not easy, it all turned out beautifully. I learned to be a student of life. I respect the way life is a teacher, and she is not always gentle.

So, how does education become a Higher Power?

I mean, I have an education, but that is not why I choose to work as a teacher. It is because I believe I am gifted by God to teach. He made a way for me to do this, most clearly, by giving me my four children and then mixing that with my unquenchable thirst for learning to teach. I become a magnet of care through my teaching. It is my way to serve the world in which I live. That is also why I write. As Brene Brown so beautifully says, "Write what you need to read." I believe that what I write needs to be read by some, maybe even desperately. If my journey to hiring and then firing many of life's supposed Higher Powers serves as a preface rather than a Post-It after the pain, then I will have served a useful purpose. For me, to write is to teach. And to do so with gratitude and grace.

But wait, Lynn. How did your education or career become your HP?

Well, for starters, I think, at times, it identified me. "I am a teacher." I often expected a possible tiny gasp or a comment that followed my announcement like I was to be admired and respected. Don't get me wrong. It is very satisfying when people ask me what I do for a living, and they acknowledge it with accolades. I appreciate the recognition, but it was often for approval. It is not now. I am simply grateful. It is clearly what I was appointed by God to do as my life's work. Because of this, when I feel like I do not want to go to work (usually in the month of March) or when I am exhausted by certain students who are unwilling to even try, I remind myself that this is my calling. It is God who purposed me to carry on. So, on those days, I act on faith, not my feelings.

Rolling back the film of my life, I again see the clips of the film where my being a teacher gave me the approval I was on a continual path to seek. The badge of honor I once again needed when I would forget who gave me my ability and my opportunity to teach. Maybe this applies to you, too.

Being an educator is a noteworthy career. It is. The academic requirements are strenuous. The hours of planning and grading feel infinite. The expectations of parents and students are enormous and often thankless. But, for me and many others, it is ultimately a work of the heart. It is a language of love and requires great care. Many careers have similar aspects, and each is essential. Essential to the worker and to those who benefit from the worker.

The year 2020 was the year of the pandemic, COVID 19. It was a year of huge change in education. No one knew what they were doing or how to do it. It's been the most difficult experience of my 18-plus years in public education. We all went home one day in mid-March only to later find out that we would not be returning to our physical classrooms until mid-October via hybrid teaching. I went from an average class of 32 students to an average of five, and in some classes, two. What's worse is that I was teaching behind plexiglass in my physical classroom, wearing a mask. I could hardly tell who my students were behind the masks they were mandated to wear.

One week, after day two of hybrid teaching, I came home, overcome by feelings of sadness and frustration. As I processed what the new way of teaching had become behind a screen, even in my own physical classroom, I wanted to quit. I could not see the value of teaching or learning in this setting.

Thankfully, I shared this with a dear friend, Nancy. She knew me so well and understood me. I am totally transparent with her and knew she would guide me toward the best direction. She would not tell me what to do but shed her own experience and then compassionately show the way by brushing away the stuff that doesn't matter so that I gain insight and confidence to take the next indicated step forward.

So, she reminded me of the whys of my career and my love for why I do what I do. She also reminded me that this particular time of life was creating fear of many unknowns for everyone. I needed to approach my life's work of teaching with grace and kindness. An authoritarian attitude mixed with fear was not going to serve me or them well. While this is often a chosen approach by many who are in positions of "knowledge" or "power," it does not serve us or those in our arena well. How right she was! Months later, in April of that school year, I was selected for a PTSA Foundation Award for

Outstanding Teacher. I was shocked. This acknowledgment showed me that when I implement my life with truths, such as knowing and acting with God as my HP, not my knowledge, I reap, and my students reap what we sow together.

Learning is a life-long journey if we allow it. Today, as I read a few daily inspirational books and began to write in my journal, I gained a new root to my tree of life. Here is what I wrote,

"Learning that God is sovereign over everything, I am aware that today is the gift. Allow today with all it brings or does not bring. Stop wishing for tomorrow. Today is the gift. Live it with purpose, and see the opportunities to love and trust God." This is how I transform into the woman He created and intended for this day.

Yes, I think I am learning some stuff.

CHAPTER 9

Alcohol (Substance Abuse)

> "You shall not make for yourself an idol (people, things, alcohol, etc.) in the form of anything in heaven above or on the earth beneath or in the waters below. You shall not bow down to them or worship them; for I, the Lord your God, am a jealous God, punishing the children for the sin of the fathers to the third and fourth generation of those who hate me."[22]

"Who has woe? Who has sorrow? Who has strife? Who has complaints? Who has needless bruises? Who has bloodshot eyes? Those who linger over wine, who go to sample bowls of mixed wine. Do not gaze at wine when it is red, when it sparkles in the cup, when it goes down smoothly! In the end, it bites like a snake and poisons like a viper. Your

---

[22] Exodus 20:4–5 NKJV

eyes will see strange sights, and your mind will imagine confusing things. You will be like one sleeping on the high seas, lying on top of the rigging. 'They hit me,' you will say, 'but I'm not hurt! They beat me, but I don't feel it!' When will I wake up so I can find another drink?"[23]

This is so challenging to read. The Bible. The authority and divine wisdom that comes from it is, as the apostle Paul says, "... For the word of God is alive and active. Sharper than any double-edged sword, it penetrates even to dividing soul and spirit, joints and marrow; it judges the thoughts and attitudes of the heart."[24] It can be read for understanding and can also be read as a form of unhealthy, fear-based conviction. I did that a lot. Not anymore. Now, I work to read it as a text of incredible love, truth, and wise direction. While I do not claim to understand the depth or breadth of it, I know it to be my greatest source of living. The Big Book of AA follows suit. It, too, is, in my opinion, inspired by God into the life of Bill Wilson for alcoholics. Both serve as my life's companions.

The synonym for alcohol is spirit. Many competing and complicated stories surround the words, all the way back to the fourth century B.C. Even Aristotle wrote about the process. It was thought that drinking put "spirits" into the drinker's body. For me, I can see how this is true. As

---

[23] Proverbs 23:29–35 NKJV
[24] Hebrews 4:12 NIV

my husband, Danny, said to me, "When you drink, you change." I did not believe him when I was actively drinking. Now, I do. It is like someone turns on a light switch when I drink. I take the first sip, and it feels so good. It is almost instantaneous, the relief. The effect is amazing. It is quick and effective. Next, I have another glass (red wine is my favorite, especially a good Cabernet), and I get fun and very social—the life of the party and very sexy. At least, that's the way I feel. And, it is how I act. It is dangerous. It is a slippery slope. It is a point of no return.

But to admit that it was an idol or my Higher Power was far too big a confession. My pride and my education prevented me from seeing it, much less confessing it. It took quite a long time for me to own this as truth. It took many years. But, as the Bible says, "You shall know the truth, and the truth shall set you free."[25]

When I first visited Twelve Step meetings as a guest, I was inspired by the sobering stories of these people. I would sit in what they call "Speaker Meetings" and listen to a member get up to the podium and say, "Hi, my name is _____, and I am an alcoholic." In unison, the audience would say aloud, "Hi, _____." It was a reassuring but awkward greeting, one that was counted on like being greeted by the bellman at the door of a hotel. Next, the speaker would unfold, in a general way, his or her

---

[25] John 8:32 NJV

experience, strength, and hope. This is the format in the Big Book of AA from Chapter 5, "How It Works." "Our stories disclose in a general way what we used to be like, what happened, and what we are like now. If you have decided you want what we have and are willing to go to any length to get it, then you are ready to take certain steps." As they shared, I would, most often, be captivated. The stories of these typically well-dressed people with tragic stories of how they reached "incomprehensible demoralization" was enough to cause anyone listening to take heed lest they go down a similar path. It was humbling to sit and hear the worst days of a person's life. The consequences of alcohol, the blackouts, debt, immorality, loss of children and spouses, DUIs, and hospital and jail time. The denial of alcohol's destructive role is almost unbelievable when I listen. All because alcohol becomes the King of the alcoholic's life. Alcohol was their Higher Power.

I felt so sorry for these seemingly normal people. How did they end up here? It baffled me. I could not imagine. I could not relate. Until I could.

My relationship with alcohol began when I was about 17. I was in high school, and "partying" was what we did on the weekends. Typically, I was the DD (designated driver), fulfilling my ever-so-familiar role of responsibility. My best friend, Kelly, and I would find out where the weekend parties were and make plans with others to go.

Drinking was not something I liked as it relates to taste. I can still remember my first drink—Bacardi rum and Diet Coke. Ewww! But the effects of alcohol were quick, and it sure spiked my curiosity to continue. Being the oldest of my four siblings and full of all that aforementioned exhausting role of responsibility was reason enough to want to escape via alcohol. But, my responsibility most often won out when I would have the opportunity to drink. Getting drunk was not my goal. Having fun, fitting in, and flirting was what I found fulfilling. It was like a key to freedom. It didn't take much effort to use it.

Most people say that, at first, alcohol is fun. Yes! I agree. But then, later, it often becomes fun with problems and then no more fun, just problems. I can say that this was my experience. While I understand the role it took in my life, when I enjoyed it and later needed it, it is an addictive substance. According to the Alcohol and Drug Foundation, "Alcohol is a depressant drug, which means it slows down the messages traveling between the brain and the body."[26] It is defined as "intoxicating" by the CDC. Since it is a drug, it might be wise to ask if there is really a safe level. Or when does it become addictive? It is a slippery slope that carries risks, as taking any addictive drug does. Society does not tell us that. Marketing and media sell a very different picture. It is a money-making, slick-looking, dangerous promise keeper.

---

[26] https://adf.org.au/drug-facts/alcohol/

It was fun, and trouble did not come from it early on, not even when I went away to college. In fact, I hardly drank in college. My roommate and I liked White Zinfandel in a box, as it was cheap, and we felt grown-up, but it was not intended for intoxicating purposes. We felt mature. As I dated men, it was more of a romance enhancer on a date. It let me release some of my inhibitions. It felt good, and I loved the effects produced by alcohol. It's kinda magical with a twist of wickedness. Little did I know how much I would grow to want it and later, much later, depend on it.

Life rolled along. I graduated college and married, and alcohol was a rare beverage. But as I wrote in an earlier chapter on my marriage, it later contributed to irresponsible and selfish decisions, and they were linked to, again, my need for love. These became decisions that I needed but became painful, and I wish I could say that alcohol was not involved. Two of my children do not speak to me today because of these decisions.

Later, alcohol became a needed and faithful friend. When my marriage was at low tide, it was what I used to ride the tide, the tide of a sad, empty marriage. Honestly, it helped me stay married. Is this good? Maybe. Maybe not. It masked reality. It bought time. It licked my deep wounds. Truly, it was the great Band-Aid. But the wound was like a terminal illness, spreading and causing me to eventually experience depression and wanting to die. That is a big statement, wanting to die, but it became true. I felt hopeless in my marriage. I remember distinctly waking up one summer morning, on summer vacation, and heading into our sunroom. I sat down and had absolutely no motivation, no energy, and no idea as to how I could keep living. I was clinically depressed. I know this because my marriage and family therapist wanted to prescribe medication for me. I said no, not yet. It sure got my attention, though. I thought one thing—if this is God's idea of life for me, I cannot do it. I really wanted to die.

I had to believe He had more for me than this way of mere existence. But, I did not know what it was or if I would ever revive myself. The truth is, I could not. Not on my own willpower.

During the last three years of my marriage, my drinking increased. A lot. I knew it but figured, "Oh well, that's the least of my problems." If you were in my home, in my situation, in my marriage, you would likely have poured me a drink or offered me a bottle. I had no idea that the drinking would lead to dependency. Total dependency. Both physically and emotionally.

I suffered from alcoholism and now know that my alcoholism was a symptom of an underlying problem. And my addiction to it distorted my awareness. It did not want me to see that I was lost and was being held as a prisoner in a cell.

My self-awareness faded with each passing year, a phenomenon that was initiated early in my life when I tried to shape myself to fit what others wanted me to be or how they wanted me to perform—aiming for perfection. It may not have been true, but it was my perspective. It dictated what I should do or shouldn't do. It filtered and blurred reality, hindering me from processing genuine feedback and keeping me from my life experiences. So, I brought a false sense of who I was or a partial me into adulthood and into my relationships. I betrayed who I was, and it erased my true self, limiting my beliefs about what I wanted and needed. It was like I was "sleepwalking," says Allen Berger, Ph.D. in his book *Emotional Sobriety*. As the years went by, I just stopped listening to myself, and the easiest way to manage that was to turn to alcohol.

If you are like me, you may be thinking, "How weird" or "How sad." I used to think that, too. My picture of a person dependent on alcohol was a man or woman who was on the sidewalk drinking out of a bottle that was stashed inside a brown bag. He or she was probably unemployed and, likely, homeless—a picture of desperation and misery.

However, during my marriage, it was absolutely my remedy. It was the force that kept me in the marriage. It wasn't until I left the marriage that I grew less needy of alcohol. Yet, by then, it was too late. I had unwittingly crossed the invisible line into alcoholism. I just didn't know it.

In fact, after my divorce, when I was asked out for a dinner date followed by a Twelve Step meeting because he was a recovering alcoholic, I felt super sorry for him and everyone else in the room. I thought, "I'm so embarrassed for these people." I could not imagine spending a Friday night in a recovery meeting. I really knew nothing more about it. And, I didn't want to know anymore. No need. But I liked him and was extremely attracted to him. So, I went. It was my first exposure to this fellowship.

Another significant nudge occurred during one of my regular Codependents Anonymous meetings when a young woman, Sophie, shared her decision to read a book called *This Naked Mind* by Annie Grace. This was when my real interest grew. Why? Well, I had great respect for this young woman for many reasons in my meeting. Sophie loved to learn and was an avid researcher and reader. Since learning is one of my highest values, I wanted to consider her own challenge, which was to consider giving up alcohol for 30 days. I was certainly curious. I had a man I was starting to date who was sober for more than 15 years and now a gal in recovery whom I really respected on the sobriety wagon. Hmmm … the confluence of influences piqued by curiosity.

I am not one to readily comply with others' suggestions or commands. It is a character flaw stemming from pride that manifests in various instances. I prefer to conduct my own research and then decide for myself what I want to do. I hate being told what to do. So, I bought the Audible version of *This Naked Mind* and began listening reluctantly. I was looking for holes. It was compelling, to say the least. I could not dispute the author's approach, her statistics, or her experiences. She reached right into my thoughts, speaking truths about alcohol to me. It was absolutely the paradigm shift I needed.

The book uses the term "alcohol-free." I wanted to try to live "alcohol-free," but I really did not think I could. I doubted my capability. I had tried. I might get a few days without alcohol, but I could not wait for it to be Friday to indulge once more. Concurrently, my body was in its most unhealthy state. For those who know me, this would cause a look at me with raised eyebrows. I am an ardent advocate for health and fitness. My weight is consistently within a two to three-pound fluctuation. I exercise four to five times a week, play pickleball, have hired personal trainers, and eat a clean, lean, and organic diet. The truth was that while I may have appeared fine on the outside, I was not. My belly was bloated, my clothes felt uncomfortable, the night sweating was horrible, and I was becoming increasingly restless, irritable, and discontent. I began to think this was normal, attributing it to approaching menopause. I merely wished for things to go my way, thinking all would be well. Most of the time, I typically got my way or figured out how to achieve what I wanted.

Each morning, I would wake up and vow to make the day different. I followed my regular devotional readings, journaling, meditating, and praying. Only to come home after a day of work all too eager to pour my glass or two of wine, particularly my beloved red wine. Initially, this started out as a Friday night celebration but escalated as life presented more challenges. It became my coping mechanism, and it worked great! The promise of alcohol is that it delivers exactly what it promises. What those attractive bottles don't tell is the lie that there is actually potential poison in a bottle. No one knows when or if that elixir will become addictive. This means that no one knows the tipping point. It is, actually, ethanol, and though not all alcohols are ethanol, all ethanol is alcohol. It is a drug, and it became addictive for me at age 53. I had a problem that I could not fix on my own. I could not, with any certainty, stop drinking on a nightly basis. I would tell myself that I would and could, but when my work day ended, and I came home after the gym - yes, it is ironic, I would pour that seemingly much-deserved glass of wine and more as time passed.

Many episodes took place that would later show up as alcoholic behavior. I just did not know how to recognize these like I do now. Dinner parties, for example, with my girlfriends were opportunities where I could see my alcoholism. The party would take place at my house; we'd have varieties of wine, a yummy collective dinner, and lots of fun. At 10:00 or so, when the gals were leaving to go home, I'd bid goodbye to the last guest. Next, I'd proceed to pour myself more wine. Not because I was thirsty. It was because I desired to sustain the effect of alcohol. It was my favorite companion—my friend. I'd hate myself the next day.

Yet, the one ugly repeating episode toward the end of my drinking was the "Friday night fight."

As a teacher, divorced at this time, I looked especially forward to Friday nights. I would have put in a long workweek and look forward to shedding the cloak of responsibility and structure. My close friend at the time, also a teacher, would welcome me over after work. I would drive over to her home about 20 minutes away with a bottle of champagne in tow, and we were off! We'd pop open those bottles, prepare a healthy dinner (we at least had that part straight), and then we'd proceed to chat about the week and laugh while consuming two to three bottles of champagne. Gradually, as the alcohol flowed, I'd start to literally wine (a short pun on words, whine) about the sober man I was dating, and I'd get all puffed up with me, finding every fault I could with him. Horrible. Then, I would drive home. I hate writing that. I really do. It was so wrong. Driving home while intoxicated, praying I wouldn't get pulled over. I deserved to get pulled over. I deserved a DUI. That is how foolish alcohol made me. It convinced me I was capable of driving. It was selfish, self-centered, and unsafe.

Upon returning home, I'd call my devoted, sober boyfriend. I would pick a fight over the phone. Poor guy. He put up with so much of my alcoholic behavior. It was terrible. Subsequently, I'd have to apologize (usually the following day), and he would forgive me. Today, I can only say that it was his understanding that I was an unwell woman that allowed him to offer me tolerance and patience. He did not have to, but he did. I know now that he prayed for me to see my alcoholism.

Crazy but true, I became angry when he was happy and helping others. He attended his 12 Step meetings and experienced the wonderful fellowship, and I'd be angry. I'd question him, attempting to find fault with him. It wasn't him; it was entirely me. I did not want to deal with my alcoholism. I felt increasingly restless, irritated, and discontent. "Misery loves company." He was "happy, joyous, and free." I was so miserable that I could not accept his joy. Instead, I attacked it. I want to put it all into words, but it is hard. It was like I was robbed of the spirit of God the more I drank. It was stealing life from me, but I was allowing the intruder in every day!

Big nudge number three also came with a considerable amount of knowledge. I had read yet another book, *The Hormone Reset Diet* by Sara Gottfried, M.D.[27] It provided further reasons why I should stop drinking, along with tons of other

---

[27] D., Gottfried Sara M. *The Hormone Reset Diet: Heal Your Metabolism to Lose up to 15 Pounds in 21 Days*. HarperCollins Publishers Inc, 2015.

great facts and tools. It was a life-changing read. In fact, I have read and reread this book via Audible multiple times, and I share it with every middle-aged woman who wants to know my "secret." It's not a secret, but an incredible health resource for women seeking education on hormones and real solutions. One of Dr. Sara's resets pertains to alcohol. Consequently, I started considering eliminating alcohol, at least temporarily. Although truth be told, it was mainly because I desired to be fit and look good! But I always found one more excuse.

On August 3, 2017, I hosted a dinner party. I had no desire to drink, yet it was all so familiar—the friends, the food, the festivities, and especially the wine. So, I did. I drank. I felt miserable the next day because I wanted to embody that flawless, perfect gal. But I could not perfect this. I was powerless.

It was the next morning that I woke up and simply knew. I had not even been intoxicated the night before. It just stopped working. It was just not fun. I had reached my bottom. Unsure what to do about how I felt, I called my sober boyfriend. He simply said, "Okay, just don't drink for today." I thought, "Okay, that sounds manageable."

The following weeks were a journey of taking "one day at a time." However, the next BIG hurdle was right around the corner—my birthday. Naturally, it called for champagne. I bought the bottle a month in advance. It was ready and waiting like an excited girl waiting for her first date to arrive.

My sweet and sober boyfriend made lovely dinner reservations at a popular hot spot for dinner. As we drove to the venue, my mind was spinning like a top. All I kept turning over and over in my mind was how to celebrate without a drink and why not have one, maybe two. After all, it was my birthday.

Upon arriving at the restaurant, a novel dining experience awaited us. The waiter, full of enthusiasm, presented us with a range of fantastic signature drink options. He then asked for our drink order. My boyfriend said, "Give us a moment, please." This allowed him to say, "Honey, if you want a drink, it's okay." Powerful. He gave me the choice. He gave me permission to drink. This was the single greatest turning point for me and led me to my decision to want sobriety. It was the first time in a long time that I went against the familiar and made the right decision for me. It was my choice. He aided me in making that choice. He also added that I could always opt not to drink today and have the champagne tomorrow.

As I write this, I sigh. It was a pivotal, precious moment.

I decided not to drink. We ordered soda water with lime and enjoyed an amazing, creative, delicious dining experience. Sober.

- -

What I really needed was human connection and love. I just did not know how to get it—perhaps because alcohol hid that need. It covered it up. It served as a false substitute.

I was about to learn, one day at a time, how to live life on life's terms as I began to replace alcohol, my Higher Power, with God as my Higher Power.

So, that is what it was like.

Strength comes next. What happened next was this … at the suggestion of my sober boyfriend, I made a phone call to a woman who was a regular attender to an open 12 Step that I had attended. It felt very awkward. I did not know exactly what I was asking her for. I was just told to call her because we might have something in common (she was a retired teacher with many years of sobriety), and perhaps she could help me. She was kind, and we met the following Sunday at a speaker meeting. Together, we read from the Big Book of Alcoholics Anonymous. It was the chapter titled "The Doctor's Opinion." As we closed our time, I thanked her, but no lightning bolts for me.

I found out about some other meetings (women's meetings) and had some interesting experiences. Some were chaotic. Some were cliquey. Some were classy. I had to find my way and get "in the middle" and keep coming back because that was what I was told.

At the same time, this gal, who became my first sponsor, and I had an agreement that I would call her everyday. I had no idea what we could possibly talk about everyday, but I did it. We also met each week at several meetings. It was like I was on a tightrope of trust. I had no idea what I was doing and felt like a fish out of water, but I kept swimming hoping I'd discover water.

One day, I did.

She assigned me to read Step One from the *Twelve Steps and Twelve Traditions* of Alcoholics Anonymous. Step One states, "We admitted we were powerless over alcohol—that our lives had become unmanageable."

Unmanageable? Me? I don't think so. "Utter defeat"? Yikes! I read on.

"Alcoholics who still had their health, their families, their jobs, and even two cars in the garage began to recognize their alcoholism. As this trend grew, they were joined by young people who were scarcely more than potential alcoholics. They were spared that last ten or fifteen years of literal hell the rest of us had gone through. Since Step One requires an admission that our lives have become unmanageable, how could people such as these take this step?"[28] Exactly! I thought.

"It was obviously necessary to raise the bottom the rest of us had hit to the point where it would hit them. By going back in our own drinking histories, we could show that

---

[28] Twelve steps and twelve traditions. (1991). Alcoholics Anonymous World Services.

years before we realized it, we were out of control, that our drinking even then was no mere habit, that it was indeed the beginning of a fatal progression."[29]

As I connected with her daily, attended several meetings each week, and worked with her on reading and working through the Twelve Steps of Alcoholics Anonymous, I began to slowly understand my relationship with alcohol and how I was maladjusted to life on life's terms. Alcohol solved that for quite a long while, but it was not working for me anymore.

Often, I hear men and women in the fellowship say, "I don't know exactly how this works, but I know that all of the tools that are suggested as a program of recovery work, and I am able to stay sober." The psychologist Abraham Maslow stated that the truth will set us free, but only if we have the courage to live it. For me, since 2017, I can say that the obsession to drink is gone. What I learned after that was how to then live without drinking. And certainly, this is a daily learning experience. Because life keeps rolling and dishing out dilemmas I must face on its terms.

So, what happens after a person gets sober from alcohol? After they are done with letting alcohol be their Higher Power? We still have alcoholism. It does not go away. It is a condition that needs, in my opinion and experience, daily maintenance. "We are not cured of alcoholism. What we

---

[29] Twelve steps and twelve traditions. (1991). Alcoholics Anonymous World Services.

really have is a daily reprieve contingent on the maintenance of our spiritual condition[30]

For me, emotional sobriety became the "next frontier." The Twelve Steps and Twelve Traditions state, "As we work the first nine steps, we prepare ourselves for the adventure of a new life ... We commence to put our A.A. way of living to practical use, day by day, in fair weather and foul. Then comes the acid test: can we stay sober, keep in emotional balance, and live to good purpose under all conditions?"[31] What a challenge this is. I know that while alcohol is no longer my Higher Power, I now know that in order to stay sober both physically and emotionally, I must maintain my spiritual condition with God on a daily basis. In fact, I need Him every hour. "Every day is a day when we must carry the vision of God's will into all of our activities."[32] As an example, I have had the tremendous and unexpected challenge of both serving and protecting my elderly parents. Serving is not so difficult, but protecting them is because, at one point, I needed armor against my three sisters in order to do this.

As I have previously shared, I am my parents' trustee. This role came with unexpected jealousy and bitterness from

---

[30] W., Bill. Alcoholics Anonymous. Fourth ed., Alcoholics Anonymous World Services, 2001.

[31] W., Bill. Alcoholics Anonymous. Fourth ed., Alcoholics Anonymous World Services, 2001.

[32] W., Bill. Alcoholics Anonymous. Fourth ed., Alcoholics Anonymous World Services, 2001.

my three sisters. After more than two years of battles with my sisters and needing the assistance of my parent's attorney, I know that through my relationships with God, my husband, my sponsor Sue, my 12 Step fellowship, and tools from the program, I can get through anything. I can even redefine family.

Even one night, as I was in a Big Book study women's meeting, I read about inventory, another tool of the program that keeps me right-sized with God. "When we habitually try to manipulate others to our own willful desires, they revolt and resist us heavily. Then, we develop hurt feelings, a sense of persecution, and a desire to retaliate. As we redouble our efforts at control and continue to fail, our suffering becomes acute and constant. We have not once sought to be one in a family, to be a friend among friends, to be a worker among workers, to be a useful member of society. Always, we always tried to struggle to the top of the heap or to hide underneath it. This self-centered behavior blocked a partnership relation with any one of those about us. Of true brotherhood, we had small comprehension."[33] I thought, "Wow!" as I read this. I underlined it. I went home and read it to my husband. He said, "That is no longer you. It is your sister."

I felt compassion towards her and my other sisters. I understood. I felt empathy. I felt grateful. It is not that I am

---

[33] W., Bill. Alcoholics Anonymous. Fourth ed., Alcoholics Anonymous World Services, 2001.

free from acting like I am the director. I know I am not, but my tools are not reliant anymore on myself and self-will run riot. I "have just now tapped a source of power much greater than [myself]" (163). I can and do call my sponsor. She is an incredible listener. She is authentic, patient, and practical. No drama. No partiality. She is practical and full of integral principles. I am honest before her, my husband, and God. Honesty is a pillar of my program. And I must constantly ask God to help me maintain honesty and be quickly convicted when I am not. "Search me, O God, and know my heart: try me, and know my thoughts: And see if there be any wicked way in me, and lead me in the way everlasting."[34] I need this verse because as I enter into these challenges, my mind goes crazy. I want to lash out, I want to defend, I want to ask them the claim they are making, and then I want the evidence to support it. I know they cannot support it, especially Biblically. But it does not matter. I am learning to practice the principles of my God and my program instead. "After all, our problems were of our own making. Bottles were only a symbol. Besides, we have stopped fighting anybody or anything."[35] My vision has changed. My definition of L.O.V.E. has changed too. I love by seeing others as children of God.

---

[34] Psalm 139: 23–24 NKJV
[35] W., Bill. Alcoholics Anonymous. Fourth ed., Alcoholics Anonymous World Services, 2001.

I choose to **o**verlook character defects. I **v**alue others as they are. I choose to **e**ncourage.

Sometimes, I learn more after the whole "show" has played out through many scenes. In the case of my family feud, after a year of protecting my parents and supporting their wishes, they decided that the pain caused by my sisters removing themselves from their lives was not worth it. So, my parents sent a group text apologizing for whatever hurt they may have caused my sisters in order to achieve peace. This was yet another experience for me to allow people to be who they are and to accept life on life's terms. The idea of "I'm right. They're wrong. So what?" made new sense to me. My dad and mom needed to do what they wanted so they could give my sisters what they wanted. And my sisters wanted their way with my parents' trust. But peace for my parents was of greater importance than being right. Oh well. I know my parents did nothing wrong, but my sisters demanded my parents apologize if a relationship was to be had, albeit twisted towards their demands. Of course, God's ways are higher than our ways. And "There are six things that Lord God hates, seven that are detestable to him: haughty eyes, a lying tongue, hands that shed innocent blood, a heart that devises wicked schemes, feet that are quick to rush into evil, a false witness who pours out lies, and a person who stirs up conflict..."[36]

---

[36] Proverbs 6:16-19 NIV

As time is the teller of what is, and God sees all, nothing is hidden from His sight, more about my sisters has since been revealed. More deceit, lies, and greed rose to the surface regarding an asset my parents shared with one of my sisters. It was like the cape of a hidden villain being ripped off. And yet, the blame was placed on my parents; it completely caught them off guard. Of course, it is all centered on their said inheritance. The other sister, equally as disguised, lied too. After telling my parents and me that holidays would be celebrated every other year, she placed my ex-husband at the forefront of these invitations and eliminated me. And then she claimed it was because I am a divorced woman. Never mind that they all attended my remarriage with enthusiasm and engaging roles on that very day. My parents have now chosen to spend these holidays with me. "You may be sure that your sin will find you out."[37] The final chapter has yet to be written on this, and I know that God will not be mocked. "Therefore, rid yourselves of all malice and all deceit, hypocrisy, envy, and slander of every kind."[38]

I know that the greatest enemies of alcoholism are resentment, jealousy, envy, frustration, and fear. So, I must choose to "grow by my willingness to identify these enemies and convert them into assets."[39] I read that my past and present

---

[37] Numbers 32:23 NIV
[38] 1 Peter 2:1 NIV
[39] W., Bill. *Alcoholics Anonymous.* Fourth ed., Alcoholics Anonymous World Services, 2001.

can become my principal asset to my family. It is, in my experience, dependent on my relationship with God and His way for me to live. It is my great possession. Alcohol is no longer my Higher Power. And that gal, the one who caused me curiosity in terms of stopping drinking, is now one of my sponsees. We do sobriety together, and it is beautiful and fulfilling because, unlike my relationship with my sisters, it is meaningful and God-driven.

CHAPTER 10

Remarriage

When I first filed for divorce in December of 2011, I was starved for love. I really had no idea what that meant because I had only known how to gain acceptance based on what I did or how I looked or performed. And for me, that equated to love.

In fact, one dear woman of great spiritual insight and Biblical wisdom said that it was like I had been eating stale bread for most of the 26 years I was married, and then, in walks Danny. He is sweet and incredibly refreshing, which is exactly what I needed.

I needed and wanted someone (especially someone good-looking) to notice me, to be drawn to me, to want me. It felt incredible. I needed someone playful, someone who would bring less "adult" into a relationship because I had way too much of that my entire life. I also needed someone who understood grace. My life had been shaped by performance, so finding a man who understood the need for grace was like placing ointment on an open wound. It felt a bit uncomfortable at the onset, but then I received it as healing and soothing. He was a warm, inviting blanket to my frightened mind and body.

So, we met, and while we experienced many struggles, the pull was one of both love and physical chemistry, and honestly, that never changed for me. I am greatly attracted to him. It was like a magnetic force of great power.

If you are familiar with the Enneagram (I think it may be worth a look as an insightful tool), I am a #7, the "Entertaining Optimist."[40] He is a #6, the "Loyal Guardian." My core desire is to be happy, fully satisfied, and content. My core fear is being deprived, trapped in emotional pain, limited or bored, and missing out on something fun. My core longing is that I will be taken care of. My core weakness is gluttony: feeling a great emptiness inside and having an insatiable desire to "fill myself up" with experiences and stimulation in hopes of feeling completely satisfied and content (Beth McCord, Enneagram Coach).[41] No wonder I have been seeking higher powers for so long! I share this information partly because it brings awareness to me and partly because I see what I need to see, am aware of it, and consider it carefully

---

[40] *The Enneagram Institute,* www.enneagraminstitute.com/. Accessed 4 Feb. 2024.

[41] *The Enneagram Institute,* www.enneagraminstitute.com/. Accessed 4 Feb. 2024.

as I navigate my life. The #6 "Loyal Guardian's" core desire is having security, guidance, and support. Their core fear is fearing fear itself, being without support, security, or guidance, being blamed, targeted, or alone, or being physically abandoned. His core weakness is anxiety, scanning the horizon of life trying to predict and prevent negative outcomes (especially worst-case scenarios), and remaining in a constant state of apprehension and worry. His core longing is to be safe and secure.

Because I am a learner by nature, it explains why I love teaching. It is how I am hard-wired, and as I read these personality types, it is obvious to me that my title of an optimist is actually a detriment at times. In my relationships, I continue to believe in the best. I believe that if I stay optimistic (and delusional), he will change. If I stay happy, then I can push down the sadness that I feel when he is perhaps acting out due to fear and then looking for me to be a safe and secure anchor. But this is a terrible fit if I want contentment and to experience care by someone, especially if I do not want to be alone. Or is it?

Each year that we were together brought more of the same. It was a cycle of me striving and believing he would care for me and that we would be happy if we just created enough fun experiences and I could settle his chaotic mind soaked in fear. He likely believed that I would be a safe and secure resting place, but I hated this feeling of responsibility.

The terrible result was multiple break-ups, engagements (x3), living together for six months, and both of us living in an ever-present state of fear. He would try and try to prevent negative outcomes, but life would present itself as it does, unbridled and challenging. And I would try to control to get the desired outcome I wanted. Crazy-making for both of us.

The cycle of intense love, then drama (based on fear), and then break-up was like a play where you know the ending.

The dysfunction of all this shows my tolerance for denial. Denial is rampant in the student population I teach. Yet, in teaching, I believe in the potential of all my students. Guess what? It is worthless. Action is. We needed to act based on faith, not fear. But we did not know how to do that without help.

I am a lover of words. For some people, they are just symbols on a page. For me, they actually cause change. I have a large poster in my class that reads, "Words don't change things, but words change people, and people change things." I believe this.

After a lot of pain, I came to understand my relationship. I love him. He is my best friend, and I am consistently exhausted by his behavior. I kept trying to change him. I was wrong.

His fear-based living and spiritual deficiency were unmanageable, and I was powerless to change it.

So, I ended the relationship. It was painful but not the excruciating pain of our prior break-ups. I knew I was making the right decision. It was clear. The poking and prodding of God through Danny's cycle of behavior was evident. I did not feel afraid. I was not in fear. I just knew. I became numb to his advances or efforts to move us forward.

I met with a dear friend, Jim, whom I greatly respect and with whom I did a lot of work. He suggested an inventory of the relationship between Danny and me. This exercise on paper showed me what I needed to do. I saw that I was in fear and was trying desperately to control the outcome of the relationship. So, I said, "God, this is not my business. It is your work to complete." I made a decision to turn it over to God. I trusted God and drew near to Him. I read my Bible, read daily devotionals, and listened to worship and praise music. I walked the beach trail, and I acted as if God was my partner and my life companion. The outcome was no longer mine. I was not the one holding on anymore. God was the one in charge. It was really painful as I let go. It was also a newfound freedom.

The results were slow, but peace came for me, and spiritual action came for Danny. He shares that initially, this was a very dark experience for him. He was angry at me, himself, and God. He "never wants to feel that way again."

While I cannot tell his story, I can tell that he wrestled with it all until he came to believe that God, and God alone, was his ultimate solution. Like I had done so many times, he made me his Higher Power. I don't say that to imply that I had any power. I did not want to be his HP, and it was clear that it did not work for us. I know that some relationships are set this way, but it causes resentment and not partnership. It means one person is driving the relationship. It does not allow for wholeness, respect, and individuality.

In my time of breaking away, I clung to the Third Step Prayer: "God, I offer myself to Thee, to do with thee as thou wilt. Relieve me of the bondage of self, that I may better do thy will. Take away my difficulties that victory over them may bear witness to those I would help of thy love, thy power and thy way of life. May I do thy will always."[42]

In the fall of 2020, we connected. He had surrendered his life to Christ while attending Calvary Chapel. His life was no longer his own as God became his true Higher Power, not me or the relationship. He gained a real feeling of freedom. He came to know the Truth, and the truths of the Bible set him free. I was very skeptical. I did not believe him. I did not want to get sucked back in, only to find out it was temporary.

He invited me to church on a Wednesday night. He was connected to God, and I could see his belief in what God was doing and what Danny believed our future was to be. He trusted. I still distrusted.

---

[42] W., Bill. *Alcoholics Anonymous.* Fourth ed., Alcoholics Anonymous World Services, 2001.

Within a few months, we were both going to mid-week church service and attending on Sundays. Danny was often scheduled to work on Sunday, but I went, and we grew. We quickly understood that we needed God to be at the center of our lives and that we were not the center of our lives. Our relationship took on a whole new definition. We then sought premarital counseling through our church and began to study what God's design for marriage looked like. We wanted it. We needed it. We believed in it. This came with some hard boundaries. Well, really one. Sex. We were challenged by our pastor to not engage sexually until our wedding. I can say that I was looking for every possible loophole. It was not easy. We fought over this a few times. Danny remained strong and became a leader as we endured the six months up until our wedding night. It was worth it. The accountability to our pastor and his regular meetings with us were very supportive. We were on our way to having a blessed marriage, one where God was the center and not our selfishness.

The wedding was beautiful. It was May 21, 2021. It took place in my parents' gorgeous backyard, and it was filled with people who we believed were saying, "Yes. Amen" to our vows and life as Mr. and Mrs. Daniel Murphy.

My husband says it like this, "The first time I saw you, I knew that you were the one. The way you looked in those jeans ... I never thought I'd deserve someone like you, and it took so long. I thought this because I never thought I was the man for you, but I knew you were the woman for me. It wasn't until I grew spiritually and became that man that you really knew you wanted that it all became possible. Now, I have everything that I ever dreamed of and everything I ever wanted. We are together forever and ever until the end. I love you so much, and I always have."

Today, we live in our simple San Clemente home with our fun Aussie Mini-Labradoodle, Bailey. We are so in love with each other and being married to one another. People notice our love. They are drawn to us as we radiate what is within us. We are a billboard for a loving marriage. It is not perfect, but we have tools and know how to get back to the basics. We love to share what God has done and is doing. It is a marriage centered on God and love. We are not one another's Higher Power. While my number one complaint is not having enough time with one another, we share a deep respect for our individual growth as a married couple. What does this look like, you may ask?

In the morning, after I prepare coffee for the two of us, we have separate quiet times. We may pray together, or we may wait until dinner time. With some more concentrated effort on both our parts, I'm praying we can increase this time. It is through praying together that we both can lay out our concerns, struggles, and praises. We can be honest before God and each other when we pray together. We then go to our respective places of work and communicate throughout our workday. He calls me on his morning drive, and we check in with each other throughout the day and often send sweet text messages as the day unfolds. Later, as he makes his way home, we connect about what time or where we will have dinner. I love to cook for him, and yet, some nights, this is not possible. We have Twelve Step meetings and mid-week church, and he has the added responsibility of a son in high school who lives with his mom, but Danny shares a great deal of the responsibilities. When we are home together later, we love to cuddle in our pjs with our adorable Labradoodle and watch a movie or something we have streamed on television. I usually am in bed by 10:00, and he is the night owl that climbs in bed a few hours later. But he always tucks me in.

As I write this, I am reminded of a few sweet gifts of marriage. Last night, he came home around 8:00 p.m., as he needed to take his son back to his mom's house. He walked up the stairs. I was waiting to greet him. I did so with a warm embrace and kiss. He said, "It's so good to come home and be wanted and welcomed." Yes. It is.

It is because we know that love is precious and a treasure. We hope to have it with one another for a long time—hopefully with health and joy equally mixed. We are a relief to one another, like a long-awaited cold drink after a hot summer day. It is not about expectation or fulfillment. No.

It is simple and easy when we stay grateful and accept one another as God created us, just as we are for that moment. When we can remember all that we have with each other and in each other, it is truly enough. We are not seeking one another as the source of fulfillment but seeking spiritual solutions from God. Sometimes, it is through one another, and sometimes, it is not. When it is not, I am given the opportunity to see if I am actually living with God as my Higher Power.

My first sponsor said, "Stop living in the wreckage of your future." So crazy and yet so true. I linger too long in the unforeseen future, and it is a waste of the present. And the older I get, the more I understand that life is truly one day at a time. It needs to be lived fully, and fear prevents that from happening, but only if I let it. Pull the stop sign out over fear. It is stopping you and me from living a full life. Seek what God is trying to show you. It is a refining process that allows us to come to Him. If I simply come to Him, I can be still and know that He is God over all of me and my circumstances. It changes my perspective.

Today, I try to go gently, to flow. I try not to react or think I need to clear items off my plate as quickly as possible. That has not served me well. It has often been in my haste that I have made mistakes because I was trying to remove obstacles rather than just take a look at them and see what I can learn from them or move along with them. I believe that infinite possibilities are available for spiritual growth, and these possibilities are often the tricky ones, the ones I least expect to learn anything from, but I can and do if I am willing. I am learning to also be okay with not having an answer. I am learning to be content. And contentment is learned.

Ah! Contentment. That needs a paragraph. I have made lots of mistakes in this arena. It is usually because I am uncomfortable with life. I used to use it as a guise for planning or being a great organizer. Ha! Now, I know it is about me wanting to ditch my restlessness, irritability, and discontentment. Take for example my plan for an expensive vacation that would take hours and weeks or even months of work. I'd pay the deposit. I'd have it on my calendar. I'd share it with friends. Escaping reality was really what it was often all about. The rippling effects were loss of time and money and sometimes disappointing friends that I would then need to make amends to for my lack of contentment. It would sting them and me. I'd subject myself to loss of deposits and then the cancellation hassles that come from my planning without seeking what was really going on with me. Or maybe a more simple example is just not feeling how I want to feel. Maybe I am discontent over the way something or someone is not lining up with my ideas. What should I do? Yesterday, I made the decision to tune into a podcast. It helped. I then sat with my journal and wrote down what I felt and then wrote what I knew as truth. For me, putting pen to paper is almost magical. It is as if I am physically and emotionally releasing the clutter. I then closed my eyes and thought about those truths and turned my thoughts towards God. This shifts my perspective. The other way for me to shift my perspective is to just reach out to call or text someone else and see how they are doing, with no agenda except them.

I just need to let go of my agenda. It is not God's agenda. "For as the heavens are higher than the earth, so are my ways higher than your ways, and my thoughts than your thoughts."[43] What a powerful few verses to ponder. Again, I am not the director. There is one. I am not Him. But my idea was that I was. I was incredibly self-centered. I now know that God is my Director and that I am His daughter, his agent. I work for Him and this is my ultimate job description. I have also learned, from my recovery, that as an ex-drinker, my sobriety depends upon my constant thought of others and how I might consider them and their needs. So, as I start my day, I read and pray over this quandary of others over self. As I then make my way into the traffic of the day, I remind myself, often audibly, "God direct my thinking and my agenda. Show me what you want me to do." It is often met with challenges, especially living in the selfish society of Orange County. People race to be first, cutting off all who are in their way, often to be met by a slew of red lights. Everyone seems to be racing and taking out whomever is in

---

[43] Isaiah 55:8–9 NIV

their way. This can lead me to make two choices: accept it or fight it. Fighting it only means, for me, losing my serenity. Why would I want to do that? That is just allowing someone or something else to steal my serenity. Time to change the channel.

CHAPTER 11

Church

As a woman in Twelve Step recovery, I hear many different perspectives on God. I won't bother to list some of them because, for me, it does not matter. I know they are relevant to the one searching, and I respect that search because I had to do mine. I can only recount my experience and the truth as I came to believe it and live it.

Are you ready?

Consider this because, if you are like I was when confronted with the idea that I was, for example, an alcoholic, I wanted to do everything I could to push that away. Confrontation didn't rank high on my list of favorites! Being labeled as an alcoholic was not even a remote possibility. Yet, after hearing many testimonials, identifying with my own version of powerlessness, and feeling restless, irritable, and discontent for days on end, months, and even years, I was finally ready to listen and take direction. I was done with who I was and the snare of fear. I hope this chapter helps direct you to God, the Higher Power. But even if it does not, or you just need to do some more "research," I do hope and pray that you will come to a richer realization: neither you nor other people, places, or things are the Higher Power. This alone can grant you freedom.

In my life, I can now see that original dot-to-dot puzzle connecting to form the finished picture. I was being weaned from other dependencies. My Higher Power wants me to be wholly His. My security is to rest solely in Him—not in other people, places, institutions or things. Sometimes, it feels like I am walking on a tightrope, but I know that a safety net is underneath me: the everlasting arms of my HP.

I love this! But I hate learning it! And it is not like I get it and then I'm good to go. Nope. It is a continual learning curve with lots of ups and downs. It's akin to playing the old childhood game of hopscotch. I throw my marker into the furthest square I hope to reach. I hop towards it, trying to balance where other markers pose as obstacles. Seeking balance, I then teeter on one leg to try and pick up my marker without losing my poise. Sometimes, I succeed. Often, I don't. I have to go back, wait for my next turn, and restart with new attempts to reach the destination.

As I have shared in all the preceding chapters of this book, *Stop the Empty Search,* I spent most of my life searching for a Higher Power—one who has all power. Sometimes, embarrassingly, I acted like it was me. It has surfaced in so many ways, all inadequate, all counterfeits. Even in churches, I did this. I thought and lived for a long time as if church was my answer. It wasn't. It still isn't. And before you are tempted to maybe get angry if you are a regular church member or even throw this book into the nearest trash can, I challenge you to carefully consider a few of my experiences. Church can be a destination for many people. It can be a destination of refuge where someone is going or perhaps is being sent or maybe just finds their way to it. It can also be a place of worship, a place to gather and grow from sound Biblical teaching, and much more.

But how did a church become my HP? It's a good question. Maybe for many of you, like me as a young girl, church was a big building with stained glass windows, lots of uncomfortable wood pews, and an ostentatious altar. Not at all approachable. It may have a man in a vestment or perhaps a cassock, a suit, or maybe even a Hawaiian shirt. In any case, for me, it started as a very formal place with lots of formalities. It was a place to be with my family every Sunday, dressed in our best and behaving our best. Later, I learned from school and neighborhood friends that there was more than one church. It was a bit of a shock. Even more of a shock when I learned later that it was not the only place to find the God of the Bible. In fact, the church of my childhood was not a place to learn much about the God of the

Bible. It was a place to learn rules, a place to learn about what to do and what not to do. It was a place I revered and also feared. It was a place of tradition. It was not a place where I learned the complete Truth.

The real shift came for me when, at 18, I met and began dating an older man who, on our first date, took me to dinner. Easy enough. But on the next date, he asked me if I would go to his church with him. I said, "Yes." Secretly, I wasn't really interested in the church part, but I was very interested in him. His striking blue eyes were enough for me to agree. So, on Easter Sunday morning, a day I would normally attend church with my family, I went with him.

It was held at an elementary school—a new church without a permanent home. It was a non-denominational church. People carried and used their Bibles. I had never brought a Bible to church; in fact, I didn't own a Bible. Now, I find it ironic to attend church without a Bible. Because what else would be used in place of the Bible? It is, as I believe now, the written word of God—fully inspired without error, the infallible word of faith and practice. It is the roadmap for my life.

But how did a church become my Higher Power? It's kind of easy to see in the beginning because, as a small child and adolescent, I just followed my parents and their religion. However, things changed later on. It all started with this good-looking date inviting me to a church where people brought, read and studied from the Bible. Suddenly,

I witnessed a relationship these folks had with God, with Jesus, God's son. I didn't fully comprehend it, but I was curious, and it seemed both valuable and important. Although I believed that Jesus was God's son and that He died on a cross, I lacked understanding of Him or much else related to religion. I just knew we did it. We were supposed to go to church.

So, I embarked on a short-lived relationship with this guy. Though it didn't last, it was enough for me to realize the authenticity of what I'd experienced. I knew that the Bible was a book I wanted to study because I wanted to learn who Jesus was and why he was sent to earth by God. It all felt so mysterious, and it begged for an answer. Plus, I observed how these people I was now spending time with eagerly studied the Bible and were different. I started going to their mid-week adult singles group meetings. I was drawn to them, and I knew something was pulling me toward them and toward God. I became a believer. But that was just the beginning.

The wacky part of allowing church to become my HP developed later. As I aged and matured, I made a conscious decision to follow God and learn about Jesus as the Savior of the world. I left the church of my youth and became a regular attendee of a non-denominational church. I brought my Bible!

Different settings and stages of my life, like college, being married, or motherhood, led me to different churches that were non-denominational, Bible-teaching churches—a multi-faceted journey. Many men and women showed me what faith in God looked like and how to cultivate a relationship with God. And some brought in fear, condemnation, and power. I now understand that these churches often strayed from the *love* letter of the Bible. It was based on their human interpretation rather than the words of God, just as they are laid out in the exact order and context as they are from Genesis to Revelation. These words are like gold-shining and bright, filled with treasure for those who seek to look long enough and deep enough.

What does that mean? It means a relationship with the God of the Bible is not based on works or anything I can do to earn a relationship with God. It is based on faith.

It is kind of like the program Alcoholics Anonymous. In the Twelve Steps, we learn from the first three steps that we are powerless over alcohol (we surrender), we come to believe in a power greater than ourselves (that is faith), and we make a decision to turn our lives over to the care of God as we understand God (faith in action). To further enforce this idea of faith, the book of Ephesians in the New Testament states, "For it is by grace you have been saved, through faith–and this is not of yourselves, it is the gift of God–not by works, so that no one can boast."[44] Many find this hard to believe. Regardless, it is true.

---

[44] Ephesians 2:8–9 NIV

We read this in the account of the thief on the cross in the Book of Luke.[45] The two criminals are hanging on their own crosses with Jesus. One criminal says to the other criminal, "Don't you fear God, since we are punished justly, for we are getting what our deeds deserve. But this man (Jesus) has done nothing wrong." Then he said, "Jesus, remember me when you come into your kingdom." Jesus answered him, "Truly I tell you, today you will be with me in paradise." So, the criminal did NOTHING to earn his way into God's kingdom, yet because he saw Jesus as God's son (by faith) and asked Jesus to remember him, he acknowledged his need for Jesus, and he was given the gift of eternal life. Wow! Out with the false notion or even some church teachings that imply we have to earn and work to be good enough to receive God's gift of heaven, eternal life. I did not know this for many years and was always thinking I had more to do or that I must behave a certain way to get in with God. It was impossible for me. No wonder I could not get an understanding of God and would turn to other higher powers.

I was locked up by the mighty god of approval.

Because my fundamental flaw was my dependency on other people, places, or circumstances to supply me with security (love), once again, I created another higher power—church. It is not. And it is not to be a form of power. It was never intended to be, as I learned yet again. It is to

---

[45] Luke 23:40–43 NIV

be one church, the body of Christ, consisting of men and women from every tribe, tongue, people, and nation. Each local congregation is an expression of that universal church. It is the belief in the spiritual unity of believers in the Lord Jesus Christ.[46]

One reminder on church fellowship comes from the Book of Hebrews, "And let us consider how we may spur one another on toward love and good deeds, not giving up meeting together, as some are in the habit of doing, but encouraging one another—and all the more as you see the Day approaching."[47] I can say that now I am a firm believer in this verse. I am mindful that a church is a wonderful place for me to go on Sunday and Wednesday (for mid-week service) to worship God, learn through the teaching of the Bible, and be in fellowship with other believers and followers of God. I need this in order to grow and be with like-minded folks. Again, because I am in the process of spiritual growth, I am on a continual journey with other followers of God, learning daily through my experiences, my study of the Bible, and relationships.

It is the same, for me, in the fellowship of Twelve Steps. In order for me to not only stay sober and treat my alcoholism, I need to go to meetings (three or more per week),

---

[46] Ephesians 4:4; 1 Corinthians 12:12–13; Revelation 5:9; Acts 2:42–47 NIV

[47] Hebrews 10:24–25 NIV

take the Steps and apply them as life unfolds, talk with my sponsor, and be of service. One tool, the Bible, is my map for seeking to learn more about God and to cultivate a relationship with Him in order to be purposeful for Him, and the other tool, equally as important for me, is the Twelve Step program. I need both to live life on life's terms—it is the perfect marriage for me.

CHAPTER 12

The Higher Power

Why does this need to find God AND become who we want to be AND how to live take SO long?

It is often painful, yet I am reminded of two truths: one from the Big Book of Alcoholics Anonymous that states, "We will not regret the past nor wish to shut the door on it," and the second from the Book of Romans in the New Testament, "... we also glory in our sufferings, because we know that suffering produces perseverance; perseverance, character; and character, hope."[48] Hope is so good. Hope is so necessary. Hope is so promising.

---

[48] Romans 5:3–5 NIV

It reminds me of one of my favorite poems:

> "Hope Is the Thing With Feathers"
> By Emily Dickinson[49]
>
> "Hope" is the thing with feathers -
> That perches in the soul -
> And sings the tune without the words -
> And never stops - at all -
>
> And sweetest - in the Gale - is heard -
> And sore must be the storm -
> That could abash the little Bird
> That kept so many warm -
>
> I've heard it in the chillest land -
> And on the strangest Sea -
> Yet - never - in Extremity,
> It asked a crumb - of me.

Similarly, one of my favorite novels of all time is *Redeeming Love* by Francine Rivers.[50] It is a beautiful story rooted and inspired by the Old Testament book of Hosea. Its central theme is the redeeming love of God toward us. We are

---

[49] Dickinson, Emily. *Selected Poetry of Emily Dickinson*. Doubleday, 1997.
[50] Rivers, Francine. *Redeeming Love: A Novel*. Multnomah, 2021.

people born with the original sin of Adam and Eve, in need of a God who can redeem us to himself, no matter what our history tells us.

According to Rivers, who once wrote secular romance books, it was as if God was saying to her, "You thought that was love–the steamy historical, romance-type love. But this is the real thing."[51]

Hmmm ... "This is the real thing." I love the real thing. I wanted it for a long time. I now have it. Keep reading—it is truly worth knowing.

So, if God's love is the real thing, then, in my search for love and meaning, unbeknown to me, I have been moving from one higher power to another my whole life, really just searching for God.

As I would continually move from one higher power to another, I would return to the empty search and even to behaviors that would trap me and doom me. Yet, an infinitely loving God pursues me, repeatedly, in spite of me. It feels far too much to fathom. That is God's grace.

And God has been running after me. His love is running after me. I just thought it was from other sources. I really did. I just kept coming up empty-handed and often broken-hearted.

What I sought in my family of origin, in my first marriage, as a mother, as a teacher, as a friend, codependent, alcoholic,

---

[51] Crosswalk.com

and more was *never* going to be satisfied without the love of the One who defines love, God. I just did not know what I did not know. Looking back, I can see the pain I suffered trying to figure this out. Honestly, it was well worth it.

And guess what? Pain does not necessarily go away. Just because I have God, and I now know He is my Higher Power, does not mean I do not suffer. Just because I am sober from alcohol (nearly seven years, as I write this) does not mean my life is pain-free. In fact, some might say it is worse. And I would say that it has been a new layer of living life on life's terms. Because even though I am sober, life is in session. It is full of unresolved problems. I am learning, by daily practice, how to live life as it is happening. Accepting it as it is dished out and then choosing to live in between surrenders with the help of God is how I do it. People often say, "God will not give you more than you can handle." I totally disagree. I *know* God gives me more than I can handle because He wants me to ask Him for help and then trust Him to help me do it. Otherwise, I do not have a need for God, and He wants a relationship with me. And with you. Just read the first few chapters of Genesis in the Old Testament. He created us; He wanted us.

It is not easy. I get lots of practice. I am continually being refined. But, now I move quickly into the solution rather than playing victim or being stuck in the problem and being driven by fear. I do not do this perfectly. But it happens a lot quicker. And I have tools.

I am now more interested in what I can contribute to life because life is for the living. And God is the giver of life. I am not interested in wasting time on fear; I am interested in living with purpose. It is definitely accomplished one day at a time. Daily, challenges arise where I am pushed and stretched like a rubber band to see if I will resist the stretching or allow it to see the direction I need to go. Sometimes I do well. Sometimes I do not. But I always know how to get back to myself and God. In fact, I was reminded today that God can be my shield. In between me and all the challenges from others is my trust in God. He is my strong shield. Nothing and no one can have the power to take my inward peace without my consent. With God, I can attain inner peace quickly in my heart and mind, as well as my surroundings. I can overcome my own crazy thinking, brainstorming, and life's arrows, knowing where my source of trust and truth lies.

It is not based on people, places, institutions, or circumstances. It is based on, firmly founded on, God. It may mean stopping and pausing when I approach a life speed bump. That's okay. I often bow, close my eyes, and say, "Help me, God. I need your help." I refuel on spiritual gasoline and take the next step. I have tools. I can pray. I can call my loving sponsor Sue. I can ask her and God for direction. I can ask my husband to pray with me, for me. I can call another sober woman or trusted friend who will not give me her puffed-up opinion but will listen, likely pray with me, and share her experience, strength, and hope. I can go to a meeting. I am NEVER alone. I do not have to be Superwoman or even pretend to be. I am not the Director. I am not Him—thank God! And when I do momentarily forget that or move into "Lynn, the Great and Powerful," I know it because I lose peace, and I feel anxious and controlling. Super ugly. No bueno. A waste of time, thinking, and purpose. Life is not on my terms, it is to be lived on God's terms. Humility is needed. Motives are checked. Agenda is adjusted.

As I read over this, I am offered the opportunity to share more specifically. And I share it cautiously because it needs to be understood carefully. For a couple of weeks, as I was journaling and praying in the morning, my spirit was a bit ruffled. It was connected to Danny, but I could not put my finger on it. So, rather than ask Danny, I do what I have learned to do—write it down and ask God for help. I know that when I do this, I get to turn it over to God and watch Him uncover it and make a way for me to be dependent on God and not myself. I get to see God be God.

Danny was asked to speak at a Twelve Step meeting. I, happily, went with him. As we were driving, we encountered a great deal of traffic. In fact, the road was blocked by the police. Danny explained that he was the speaker at a meeting and that we needed to get through if that was possible. They heard him and let us proceed down the blocked road. We arrived safe and sound, and the meeting began on time. He began sharing how spiritual he was and how unspiritually fit I was—he did it three times. It was the most painful experience I have had in a long time. I felt so hurt. My head said, get up, grab your purse, and go. Go! I thought about it a couple of times. I wanted to just cry. Then, my mind started filling up with the Third Step Prayer ... "Take away my difficulties, that victory over them may bear witness to those I would help of Thy Power, Thy Love, and Thy Way of life ..." I thought of the words integrity, dignity, and character. Then, as others shared in this meeting, they told him how taken back they were, how he publicly embarrassed me, and how they did not see nor know me to be spiritually unfit. They claimed the total opposite. Then, he announced that he wanted me to share. What? My mind went like a flash of lightning to "Help me, God." Help me to share with integrity, dignity, and radiant the principles of this program. Help me practice the principles "in all my affairs" as I have learned here in this fellowship of like-minded men and women. Fortunately, we ran out of time. But, as I sat there and listened to God and my program in my head, I was able to stand tall and receive the kindness of each one who came up to me baffled by what Danny said. I overcame it all with the help of God.

Yes, a conversation was held between us in the car. He made some excuses coupled with an apology, not forgiveness. I listened and challenged him with Luke 6:45, "Out of the heart the mouth speaks." We made our way to the next recovery meeting. Yes, two meetings in one evening. The second one is faith-based, so as we entered the room, I allowed the worship music to minister to me. I was reminded that Jesus was rejected, hated, and spit upon, and He did it all for me. I am able to forgive, offer grace and learn that Jesus is my everything. It will never be Danny. It was never supposed to be him. He is not my HP. In the meantime, I continued to pray. I prayed he would seek God and His Spirit would teach Danny and show him the holiness of God and the beauty of his life because of all that God has done for him.

When we arrived home, I communicated that I was hurt and that I needed time and sleep. So, we said our goodnights and I gave my sleep to God hoping the next day would bring hope. I went to work that next day, and with every text or phone call from him, I felt numb. Just numb. Danny even came in after his day with white roses and a card. I thanked him but felt zero. I called my sponsor who was livid at his behavior, and after we talked, she suggested a conversation needed to take place between the two of us–roses and a card were not enough. I was clear with her that I was not trying to punish him; I just didn't have words or feelings to cope with his words about me, especially publicly. She got it. I felt totally understood.

Our routine on a Wednesday night is mid-week church. He was preparing to go ahead of me as he is a greeter. I let him know that I had spoken to Sue, my sponsor, and that she suggested we have a conversation—that what happened deserved it. He wanted to talk right then, but I looked at the clock, 6:26, and he needed to leave at 6:30. I said it would need more time. So, we agreed to wait until after church.

As I walked up to the church doors, I heard the worship. I didn't even want to sing. I was really only there because it is what I know to do. I go by faith. It is not always because I feel like it. It was a good thing I did. I heard the music and the lyrics. "He is more than faithful." "Who am I to decide what the Lord can do?" Then, our pastor began teaching on 1 Kings 8. I listened. I asked God to show me what He needed me to see. It was this: be faithful to Danny, love him, show him how God is faithful. Next was the whispered message that I was not a victim in this situation. I am the vessel that God is using to help Danny learn what God needs him to learn. This was not about me. This is for Danny. My role was to gently ask Danny what was going on with him in his heart. WOW! It was a huge revelation to me.

So, when we came home, I shared what I heard and what I had spiritually experienced with God. I spoke about the commitment we have to God and to one another, to our marriage. I shared how his words broke my heart but God had warned me earlier in my journal and prayer time that there was an obstacle. And, we are in this together, and that iron sharpens iron. We have great purpose as a married couple. We cannot allow the Enemy a seat at our table. I learned, again, that God is THE Higher Power. God does for us what we cannot do for ourselves, but we must invite Him into our lives, our struggles, and our pain. We need to praise Him through all of it. He shows us that He is God and He will make a way out and use us, in spite of ourselves, for His good. Danny received all of it. He understood, and he asked me to forgive him. He shared deeply and I heard his cry and felt his love. This is just one of many opportunities for God to refine me.

Once I learned and believed that God is **The** High Power, I needed to get some evidence behind my claim. As a high school English teacher who teaches the power of argument in writing, it is essential! If not, I would score an F on the essay—it must be supported with evidence.

I learned that:

1. God is the Alpha and the Omega—He always existed; He is the Creator of heaven and earth (Revelation 22:13, Genesis 1:1).
2. God is Spirit, light, *love*, and truth; eternal, almighty, infallible, and unchangeable, infinitely wise, just, and

holy (John 4:24, 1 John 1:5, 1 John 4:7–8, Genesis 49:25, Genesis 31:23, Proverbs 30:5, James 1:17, Proverbs 2:6–11, 1 John 1:9, 1 Samuel 2:2).
3. God eternally exists in three persons: Father God, Jesus the Son, and Holy Spirit (Matthew 28:19).

For those of you reading who *are* Christians, this may be easily believed by you. It was for me, at least in my mind. It made sense to me by faith. BUT I did not know, really know, how to transfer this into my heart and life. So, that means that knowing is not enough. It needs to become practical in daily living. Where I actually trust this and live like it is true. Lots of people are versed in the Bible and may be great to play Bible trivia with, but that does not mean they apply it or that it shows up in their daily lives. They may, in fact, be the "hypocrites" we often label as such because that is how they act. They may be the greatest judges in your life. Don't waste time on them or their empty words. Move on and away from them. Pray for them. Chances are that they are living with the blinds partially closed or maybe even under the tutelage of a church leader who is teaching without context or verse by verse, chapter by chapter. It would be like reading a story without all the necessary characters, backstory, development, climax, falling action, or resolution. All are needed to make it complete and accurate.

Furthermore, being well-versed in the Bible is worthless if not grounded in peace and love. But that happens when you believe it to be true, act on it, and trust it.

For those of you reading who are not Christians or have not made a decision to place your life in God's hands and trust in His gift of salvation, I want you to give careful consideration to this decision. It is the most important decision you will ever make, especially in terms of your eternity and how you will live out the rest of your life—with meaning and purpose. Many just hear it and then give a number of reasons why they do not make the commitment or maybe see it as essential.

This is true of many alcoholics when given the message of Twelve Step Recovery. I did that. I had so much looking on the outside that I could not imagine needing to confess I was an alcoholic. If you are a person of wealth or societal substance, perhaps this relates to you. When we have what we need, like I had a home I owned, a BMW in my garage, a good-looking boyfriend, an amazing career, and a host of friends, why would I need to admit I am an alcoholic and give up drinking? I would not. I didn't see the need. Furthermore, I did not want to. But, as I aged and my drinking increased, I became aware that I had a problem with alcohol, that it was negatively affecting me, and that I could not stay sober on my own merits. That it had, in fact, become a god. I needed to be rescued. Similarly, as we age, we usually come to grips with questions about heaven. And we should. It is a very real conversation we should have with ourselves because we cannot save ourselves. We don't get to write the rules about eternity. We are not the creator of the universe. Even Pilate asked the crowds, "What shall I do, then, with Jesus who is called the Messiah?"[52] What will you do with Jesus?

How do you know where you will spend your eternity?

If we are to be saved from sin and have a place in God's kingdom, heaven, with Him forever and ever, we must accept God's way, not our way, a group or institution's way, or the world's way of salvation. It is not a threat to your life—it is a loving invitation to your life now and after you leave this crazy world and finally enter into God's presence.

And the alternative is tragic. It is hell. People use the word liberally, but it is a place of eternal separation from God. I hate to even write that—the hell part. But, it would be unloving of me not to tell the truth. It is very real, and just as it is real to hear an alcoholic share that they cannot ever pick up a drink again or they will die, it is the same with our eternal destiny. A decision must be made. And like me admitting I was an alcoholic and standing up to identify as one, I had to if I wanted to get sober and stay sober. A decision is required.

How does this happen?

---

[52] Matthew 27:22 NIV

Step One: Believe.

We must believe God exists and that He rewards those who seek Him. This means that you need to have a willingness to believe, by faith, that God exists. The apostle Paul wrote in the Book of Romans, "Faith comes from hearing the message, and the message is heard through the word of Christ."[53] We hear the words of Christ when we read the Bible.

Step Two: Repent

This step is the one that leads to a change in life. It is like Step 4 and then Step 9 in recovery. "... God's kindness leads us to repentance."[54] And it is followed by John 1:9: "If we confess our sins, He is faithful and just and will forgive us our sins and purify us from all unrighteousness." And He wants to forgive us because He loves us. "For God so loved the world that He gave His one and only Son, that whoever believes in Him shall not perish but have eternal life."[55]

Repentance is kind of a big deal. It has to move my ego out of the way and get me to admit that I need repentance and that I am sorry for my sins (acts against God). It is more

---

[53] Romans 10:17 NIV
[54] Romans 2:4 ESV
[55] John 3:16 NKJV

than sorrow. It is more than fear that drives me to it. It is knowing that I grieve God's heart when I make decisions that separate me from Him. I am not able to cover the sins by just trying harder or being good again. There is a price to be paid for sin. It is like the price we pay for stealing. We have to make restitution—to pay back what we took.

In the Old Testament, the price for sins was an animal blood sacrifice. I don't know why. I just know that that was what was required by God. If you read the Old Testament, you will see it over and over. What a bloody mess that must have been! Thankfully, when God sent his only son, Jesus, to die for us once and for all as the final sacrifice for sin, the OT way was no longer needed. Jesus paid that debt for us. It was not cheap, but it was enough.

Step Three: Confess

The next step in becoming a Christian is confession.

"Are you thinking that you will escape God's judgment, you who judge those who do such things and then do the same things yourself? Or do you have so little regard for his rich kindness, his restraint, and his patience that you ignore the fact that the purpose of God's kindness is to lead you to repentance? As a result of your stubbornness and your unrepentant heart, you are storing up wrath for yourself on the day of wrath, when God will reveal his righteous judgment." [56]

When we truly repent and confess, God forgives us.

It may not feel like that is enough, but this decision and action are enough. It is not based on how we feel, but it is based on what we believe about God.

Three simple steps: Belief in God. Repentance of my sins. Confession. A simple prayer to God, including the above three steps, is all it takes.[57]

Are you skeptical?

Often, I hear people say that Christians are hypocrites and judgmental. True. It is also true of all other forms of religion. But that does not give us reason to not need a Savior or to make an excuse for living life our way instead of God's way. It's not that once you become a Christian, you will not sin. It does mean that you know that God sets the standards. They are laid out for us to follow in the Bible. Just like a parent does for his child. A good parent sets up standards and establishes a way of living for their child. Why? Because

---
[56] Romans 2:3-5 EHV
[57] *Home Page*, bibleinfo.com/. Accessed 4 Feb. 2024.

of love. Unrequited love. Sometimes, that needs to come with a healthy dose of fear to establish respect or even painful consequences. However, it is to be motivated by love and usually understood through experience over time.

In the Twelve and Twelve, Tradition Nine states, "Great suffering and great love are AA's disciplinarians; we need no others."[58] I love this. As I read it, I absorb its truth.

Suffering, for me, usually comes in the form of fear. A lack of trust in a loving God as I understand Him.

When I am running the "show," it is because I want control. I want control because I am afraid of outcomes. I do not trust God when I am in fear.

My basic problem is self. My sponsor, Sue, says this to me when she is feeling "funky," this idea that we are self-absorbed. It is most likely us playing God and wanting center stage. This is written on page 62 of the Big Book of Alcoholics Anonymous. "This is the how and why of it. First of all, we had to quit playing God. It didn't work." Well, I can definitely attest to that. It goes on to say, "He is the Father. We are His children." When I ponder this, truly ponder this,

---

[58] Alcoholics Anonymous World Services, Inc. Twelve Steps and Twelve Traditions. Alcoholics Anonymous World Services, 1989.

it brings me to that precious place of how, as a mother, I love my own children. When they were very young, I can easily recall loving them so much and doing everything to care for them, to protect them, and to guide them. God does this for me, for you. He is a good, good Father. Why would a child of a loving parent not act as if this is not true?

Lots of reasons for this come to my mind. Maybe for you, too. It is often us importing onto a perfect God our experiences from imperfect parents, pain, wacky theology, and unhealthy church cultures, to name a few. It is not easy to accept these and be willing to let go and choose to view God as He really is—a God who defines love.

The band MercyMe[59] has a powerful song called "Let Yourself Be Loved." Out of respect for copyright restrictions, I cannot write the lyrics here, but I would highly recommend you look it up and purchase the song! They speak so clearly of God's love.

Letting yourself be loved is not easy in a world that gives us messages of counterfeit love. I see it all the time, especially in the halls of the high school where I teach. It is not well-defined. Love needs a definition. It requires it if we are seeking it. But seeking it means we need to know the real from the false.

---

[59] MercyMe.org

Let me give an example. When I was about 18, I began working as a bank teller. Part of the training was to recognize counterfeit one-hundred-dollar bills. One might think that the identification of these would be through the study of counterfeit bills. Not so. We were to study, touch, read, and know what a real bill was in order to know if it was counterfeit should one come across the teller window. This applies to love as well. Until we know real, true, genuine love, we may end up with a false version. This is sure to end in pain. Suffering again becomes the disciplinarian.

The apostle John wrote, "Dear friends, let us love one another, for love comes from God. Everyone who loves has been born of God and knows God. Whoever does not love does not know God because God is love." He goes on to support this love. "This is how God showed his love among us: He sent his one and only Son into the world that we might live through him. This is love: not that we loved God, but that he loved us and sent his Son as an atoning sacrifice for our sins."[60]

So, since God is love, we need to know God if we want real love. But wait a minute, you might be saying. How do I know that this definition is true? A simple Merriam-Webster definition states love is a noun: "(1) · strong affection for

---

[60] 1 John 4:7–10 NIV

another arising out of kinship or personal ties. maternal ; (2) · attraction based on sexual desire : affection ..."[61]

The above definition is very basic and a lot easier to obtain if we only want what is suggested here as the meaning of love.

I believe that a lot more, way more, to this definition exists and is wanted. But it is an empty search until, as I have written, you know that your first and foremost source of it is God. Because He is love.

Clearly, I spent the majority of my life, from childhood until I was about 50, seeking it. It wasn't until I filed for a divorce, later on admitting I was an alcoholic who needed help, and understood that love was to first be defined by God that I could receive love and be clear about what love really is. It certainly did not come from the sources the world presented to me.

It seems absurd. But is it?

When my students write papers for my class, I often write "OE" on them. This is my code for "opportunity to elaborate." I also say, "Don't tell me. Show me." I want to understand what they are trying to say through their elaboration. Explain it to me. Give me a visual so I can see what they are trying to say. If it is an argument paper, I will teach them to make a claim and then back it up with

---

[61] "love" Merriam-Webster.com. 2024. https://www.merriam-webster.com (23 May 2024).

evidence or support. Why? Because we need it to be credible. If not, it is simply opinion. Period. And while we individually may be very tied to our opinions, it really does not matter if we cannot back them up. Sometimes, when I really see the need to challenge my students, I courageously write, "Why does this matter?"

The same is true for you and me when confronted with who the real Higher Power is. Are you aware of who it is? Have you stopped at any point in this book and reflected on your own need for God as your Higher Power? "Who do you say that I am?" Matthew 16:15 is the most important question ever asked.

How is God saying "Here I am" to you? How many higher powers do you need to "worship" until you see the one worthy of your ultimate affection? In what unique ways has God reached out to you so you would notice Him?

This makes me think about my stepson. Last night, he had his first date to a formal high school dance. He went to great lengths to creatively ask the girl. With the help of his friends, they used 400 battery-operated candles that spelled out "Homecoming?" on a bluff overlooking the ocean. So sweet. She accepted. Then came the night of the big event—a suit, the flowers, and the photo shoot. But, as the dance unfolded, his date became focused on a friend of hers who was in the middle of her own boyfriend drama, leaving my stepson to instead leave his expectations of a romance into the hands of his friends and dance the night away without her. He felt sad and disappointed. She ended the relationship a day later. It hurt him.

Why do I share this? I see it as painful for him, and yet the silver lining is perhaps an opportunity to begin the lessons of God, allowing him to see that this girl, or any other girl for that matter, will never be enough to fill the one who knows what he needs and how his need for love and connection needs to come from God. And yes, it can come through other people, but ultimately, God allows many moments for us to recognize Him as the HP. My need is God's opportunity.

Let me add one more very important detail that can cause many people to walk away from choosing God as their Higher Power. Jesus. Yes, Jesus. It is almost an uncomfortable name for people. I do understand it. It often comes with reference to "Jesus Freak" or "Bible-thumping," especially in reference to the 1970s. But, as it turns out, I am a student and facilitator in an international, non-denominational Bible study and we are studying the Book of John in the New Testament. I read in Chapter 5 that, essentially, no one can honor God the Father without giving honor to His Son. Jesus's union and equality with His Father signify His worthiness to receive honor. To reject Jesus is to turn away from the Father because Jesus provides the only way to God. God and Jesus cannot be separated. Some people comfortably think about God but stumble over Jesus, whose death confronts their sin and demands a response. You cannot know God without receiving Jesus Christ as His Son and your Savior.

No matter how you have heard God's voice (a whisper, an inkling, a prompting, a closed door, an open door ...), when you decide He is your Higher Power, the search will end in love. And you will no longer be empty ever again! You may have feelings that come and go about God, but that does not mean that you rely on them. Feelings, I heard, are like clouds; they come, and they go. Truth never changes. Jesus is the way, the truth, and the life.[62]

This is your opportunity to do it. This is your opportunity to stop the empty search. This is your opportunity to be free from the weight of the world and all the false options it slips and dazzles in front of us.

If I could go back in time, I would want to know that while I knew of God early on in my life, I did not fully know that He was above all the other higher powers I sought after. I did not KNOW He was enough. I did not KNOW He was the definition of love because of who He is and what He has done for me. He is now. And when I have a relapse over this or a situation that throws me into panic or pain, I can feel it,

---

[62] Holy Bible, New International Version®, NIV® Copyright ©1973, 1978, 1984, 2011 by Biblica, Inc.® Used by permission. All rights reserved worldwide.

I can process it, and I can come to God and put Him in the middle of it for the direction He next wants me to take. It is laboring like giving birth to a baby. It often comes in painful waves that rise and fall; some of the contractions are long, and some are short, but the end result is a miraculous gift. If I submit to the process and trust the outcome to God, I gain peace and a relationship that is not just for the here and now, the temporary, but for eternity. My perspective changes. The power is shifted.

My search is over. All those titles I write about are distant labels from the past. Now, I get to practice, often, what I now know to be true. There is so much that is true and God is my source of all truth. His title is more than enough.

APPENDIX A

Repentance, Sorry, or Restitution?

Just when I thought I was finished writing … It became clear to me that many people do not know or understand repentance. It is not just "I'm sorry."

It needs to be followed up with a very important question. "Will you forgive me for _____?" I know that many people are unwilling to repent. They continue to point fingers and place blame on others. So, it is as if God said to me that maybe readers need to understand what Biblical repentance is. If my own sisters, who are church-going, BIble-toting Christians, fail to repent in an effort to restore, then it would seem clear that repentance as God defines it is a valuable point to include.

One of the things that my sisters are deceived by is perspective. They see situations from only their perspective or pain, not God's. This is sad, and I can only offer mercy toward my sisters. They do not practice the process of BIblical reconciliation.

When reading the Biblical process of forgiveness, reconciliation is not first. It is repentance. To say, "Will you please forgive me for_____?" Without this admittance and ownership, there is no reconciliation. There is therefore no restoration.

Jesus told the paralytic, "Child, your sins are forgiven."[63] When a sinful woman bathed Jesus' feet with her tears and wiped them with her hair, Jesus said, "Your sins are forgiven."[64] When a woman caught in adultery was brought before him, he said, "...I do not condemn you." [65] And as Jesus hung on the cross, he told the repentant criminal hanging next to him, "Truly I tell you, today you will be with me in paradise."[66] He followed up with the woman caught in adultery to essentially go and sin no more. He did not say, "Now you must make an effort to knock down doors," as my one sister said after forgiveness was sought. It is not a continual need to beg for forgiveness. It is once. Then, we live out our lives as humans, one day at a time, asking God to help us each day by seeking His help and will. He asked them to live their lives as a living amends for his glory. This living amends is personal.

[63] Mark 2:5 NKJV
[64] Luke 7:48 NKJV
[65] John 8:11 NIV
[66] Luke 23:43 NIV

It is between them and Jesus—according to the will and directions of God and their relationship with Jesus. It is not one we get to judge.

Even more compelling is the way that Jesus forgave those who sinned against him directly. After the Roman soldiers had scourged and nailed him, Jesus prayed, "Father, forgive them" (Luke 23:34). After the resurrection, Peter had denied him. The others had deserted him. When Jesus entered the Upper Room, they were met with divine compassion. Jesus said not once but three times, "Peace be with you" (John 20:19, 21, 26). He did this with Peter, too. After he denied Jesus three times, Jesus reinstated Peter by asking him (after the resurrection), "Simon, son of John, do you love me more than these?" Peter was hurt, the Bible says, because Jesus asked him three times in a row! The beauty in this dialogue is that Jesus gave Peter the opportunity to restate three times what he denied three times. I love this!

Dear reader, please do what Jesus models and requires of us when asking for forgiveness. It is for our own good and for our relationship with God. Your perspective is of little significance. Your perspective is just that, your perspective. It is not the Biblical process as Jesus teaches us. Pray that it changes for your own relationship with God and others.

When the Old Testament prophet Micah speaks about the Lord's case against Israel, he asks what is required of him. He is told, "To act justly and to love mercy and to walk humbly with your God."[67] Pondering this is not only needed, it is instructed. Do just that, whether others want to believe it or not. Whether they will accept it or not. We do not answer to them but to the Lord, Jesus. And we will continue to do that. Only God truly knows our hearts. We do not owe anyone any further explanation.

Life is short. This statement is Biblical. "Yet you do not know [the least thing] about what may happen tomorrow. What is the nature of your life? You are [really] but a wisp of vapor (a puff of smoke, a mist) that is visible for a little while and then disappears [into thin air]."[68]

I am blessed to be clear on this and to live my life as a sober woman, an honored wife, devoted daughter, and servant of the most high God, and with great purpose regardless of what others choose to believe or say about me. I implore you to do the same. Because your relationship with God is worth it and your relationship with yourself is worth it.

---

[67] Micah 6:8 NIV
[68] James 4:14 AMPC

ACKNOWLEDGMENTS

Thank you to my writing coach, Karen Pina at selfpublishing.com, whose time, expertise, and kindness pushed me onward.

Thank you, Sky Rodio Nuttall, my editor, who answered every question and whose expertise was needed and wanted.

Thank you to Si Herbers, my photographer who captured my personality and our friendship in my author photo.

Thank you to all who are in this book. Each of you has taught me by who you are. This has influenced how I came to be the woman I am today and how I found my ultimate Higher Power.

Thank you to my dear parents, who continued to ask about this work and wanted to see its completion.

For granting me haven, emotionally, my dear sponsor, Sue.

I am forever grateful to my husband, Danny, who understands and knows me beyond the words and tirelessly guides and supports me. He is my greatest fan and prayer partner.

Finally, and most importantly, I thank God. He is my Everything!

Thank you for reading my story.

My hope is that *Stop the Empty Search* - Come Face to Face with the Real Higher Power left an impact on you and challenged you in your own search for a Higher Power. I hope it inspires you to develop or deepen a personal, intimate relationship with God. Perhaps you are now ready to check out my website and connect more. I plan on writing and speaking more with God's help.

lynnkmurphy.com

Every review matters to me, can I count on you to leave a review so that others may want to read this?

Please head over to Amazon to leave a review or scan this QR code.

With humility and gratitude,
Lynn K Murphy

Lynn K Murphy

Scan the QR code

ABOUT THE AUTHOR

Lynn Murphy's debut memoir, *Stop the Empty Search-- Come Face to Face with the Real Higher Power*, is an extension of her love for literature and all things true to life. Her love for writing leads to prose in the areas of family, recovery, God, awareness, acceptance, and change. Lynn's philosophy will lead the reader to develop faith, hope, honor, and gratitude. Lynn is a public speaker and a high school English teacher. She earned her BA from Westmont College and her M. Ed., from Vanguard University.

She lives in San Clemente, California with her husband, Danny, and their sassy mini-labradoodle, Bailey.

Made in the USA
Middletown, DE
21 January 2025

69478517R00116